The media's watching V
Here's a sampling of our

"For those hoping to climb the ladder of success, [Vault's] insights are priceless."
– *Money magazine*

"The best place on the web to prepare for a job search."
– *Fortune*

"[Vault guides] make for excellent starting points for job hunters and should be purchased by academic libraries for their career sections [and] university career centers."
– *Library Journal*

"The granddaddy of worker sites."
– *U.S. News & World Report*

"A killer app."
– *New York Times*

One of Forbes' 33 "Favorite Sites"
– *Forbes*

"To get the unvarnished scoop, check out Vault."
– *Smart Money Magazine*

"Vault has a wealth of information about major employers and job-searching strategies as well as comments from workers about their experiences at specific companies."
– *The Washington Post*

"A key reference for those who want to know what it takes to get hired by a law firm and what to expect once they get there."
– *New York Law Journal*

"Vault [provides] the skinny on working conditions at all kinds of companies from current and former employees."
– *USA Today*

VAULT
> the most trusted name in career information™

VAULT CAREER GUIDE TO BIOTECH

VAULT CAREER GUIDE TO BIOTECH

CAROLE MOUSSALLI
AND THE STAFF OF VAULT

For information about permission to reproduce selections from this book, contact Vault Inc., 150 W. 22nd St., 5th Floor, New York, NY 10011, (212) 366-4212.

Library of Congress CIP Data is available.

ISBN 1-58131-268-7

Printed in the United States of America

ACKNOWLEDGMENTS

Thanks to everyone who had a hand in making this book possible, especially Marcy Lerner, Ed Shen, Kelly Shore, Tyya Turner and Elena Boldeskou. We are also extremely grateful to Vault's entire staff for all their help in the editorial, production and marketing processes. Vault also would like to acknowledge the support of our investors, clients, employees, family, and friends. Thank you!

Use the Internet's
MOST TARGETED
job search tools.

Vault Job Board

Target your search by industry, function, and experience
level, and find the job openings that you want.

VaultMatch Resume Database

Vault takes match-making to the next level: post your resume
and customize your search by industry, function, experience
and more. We'll match job listings with your interests and
criteria and e-mail them directly to your inbox.

Table of Contents

Visit Vault at www.vault.com for insider company profiles, expert advice,
career message boards, expert resume reviews, the Vault Job Board and more.

VAULT CAREER LIBRARY

xi

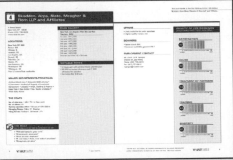

Introduction

What is Biotechnology?

"Biotechnology," or "biotech" for short, refers to the application of biological research techniques to develop products and processes using biological systems, living organisms, or derivatives of organisms. Biotech processes have been used for thousands of years, yet the industry we know today is scarcely more than a quarter century old. Bread, cheese and beer – all products made from microorganisms – have been part of the human diet for 6,000 years. But it was not until the 1970s that scientists began to apply components of these microorganisms at the molecular level to solve human problems in spheres ranging from medicine to agriculture and industry. Due to this breadth of applications, the term "biotechnology" gradually gave way to the more accurate "biotechnologies" or a collection of techniques that apply cellular and molecular characteristics and processes to solve human problems. Such techniques are applied at the molecular level and include genetic manipulation, gene transfer, DNA typing and cloning or microorganisms, plants and animals. Biotech products or "biologics" as they are sometimes called, thus originate from living organisms – bacteria, cells or animals.

Visit Vault at www.vault.com for insider company profiles, expert advice, career message boards, expert resume reviews, the Vault Job Board and more.

VAULT CAREER LIBRARY

1

THE SCOOP

Biotech Industry Overview

CHAPTER 1

History of Biotech

The biotechnology industry has experienced phenomenal growth over the last 25 years. But its beginnings can be traced all the way back to 1750 B.C., when the Sumerians used yeast to brew beer. As early as 500 B.C., the Chinese used mold as an antibiotic. In the 1860s, the monk Gregor Mendel worked on gene transmission in plants, initiating the study of genetics.

An agricultural engineer coined the term "biotechnology" in 1919. In 1928, penicillin was discovered. In 1941, George Beadle and Edward Tatum posited the "one gene, one enzyme" theory, which held that genes are coded instructions for building proteins. In 1944, Oswald Avery found that the molecule, DNA or deoxyribonucleic acid, was the molecule that contained genes. In 1953, working at Cambridge University in England, James Watson and Francis Crick discovered the helix-like structure of DNA.

The following two decades – from 1960 to 1980 – saw a rapid acceleration in knowledge. The first synthetic antibiotic was available in 1960. The first mouse-human cells were fused in 1965. In 1967, Marshall Nirenberg and Har Gobind Khorana cracked the genetic code. By the 1970s, methods to cut and paste genes were developed. By 1981, the first transgenic animals were bred.

By 1983, the first artificial chromosome was made, followed rapidly by genetically engineered plants in 1985, the use of microbes to clean up environmental pollution (oil spills) in 1986, and the first patent for a genetically altered animal in 1988.

The first non-viral full gene sequence was completed in 1995, followed by the unveiling of the cloned sheep "Dolly" in 1997, and the near completion of mapping of the human genome in 2002.

This dizzying acceleration of knowledge has created a burgeoning industry with an increasing number of commercial products that is poised to undergo significant growth in the remainder of the decade and onward in the 21st Century.

The pace of commercialization of biotech applications comes into perspective when we compare the elapsed time between development of different products and their date of commercialization. The pen was first invented in

1888 and went into production in 1938 for an elapsed period of 50 years. Television was invented in 1907 and reached consumers in 1936, a period of 29 years. Transgenics plants (such as corn adapted to resist common pests) – the first biotech products – were first created in 1983 and came to market as recently as 1994, or 11 short years. The time to commercialization has thus been significantly compressed, leaving some observers to wonder whether society has had enough time to think through the complex issues biotech innovations introduce. The growth in bioengineered products and techniques makes this an exciting time to be thinking about and preparing to get into the biotech industry.

Biotech Basics

All biotechnology techniques are based on the science of genetics, which is based on the DNA molecule. DNA is composed of sugar, phosphate and four nitrogenous bases or nucleotides: adenine (A), cytosine (C), guanine (G) and thiamine (T). Think of DNA as two long strands of string made up of sugar and phosphate groups and held together by pairs of bases in different combinations (e.g., A-C, G-T, A-G, etc.). Now think of those four bases – A, C, G and T – as four letters of an alphabet, a genetic alphabet. Finally, imagine those bound strands as twisted together into a helix shape and you have a mental image of DNA. Watson and Crick used a technique called x-ray crystallography to visualize the structure of DNA back in the late Middle Ages of genetics – that's about 1953, as we said above. They won a Nobel Prize for this discovery. Today, human DNA can actually be visualized and photographed.

Apart from water, the predominant component, human tissues are made up mostly of proteins. The proteins that make up the traits that make you and I different – hair color, height, eye color, etc. – are based on differences in the sequences of nucleotides along our genes. Each gene codes for the construction of a different protein, so even though we do not actually see genes, we do see the products for which they code. Proteins vary by type, number and order of amino acids and come in two varieties: Structural proteins (e.g., collagen, elastin) give shape to human tissues, and functional proteins (e.g., hormones, enzymes) carry out the cell's tasks or metabolic functions. Genes have different sizes and come in different sequences. This means that the number of letters or nucleotides varies as well as how these nucleotides are ordered along a section of DNA.

> **Biotech factoid:** Proteins are composed of twenty (20) different amino acids held together by peptide bonds. The human body contains over 100,000 proteins!

OK. So you have four letters of the alphabet to code for 20 amino acids, which somehow produce over 100,000 proteins. Nirenberg and Khorana, who are not nearly as famous as Watson and Crick, figured out that that bit of DNA magic happens by way of "codons." The alphabet (aka nucleotides or bases) gets "translated" in groups of three; each three-nucleotide group is thus a codon. Arranging four nucleotides in groups of three means that there are 64 different arrangements or 64 different codons. With only 20 amino acids to code for, there are enough codons to do the job. If you're curious about the math steps we've skipped over, you're probably already aware of how fascinating human life is organized.

The upshot of this abbreviated genetics lesson is that biotech products are based on DNA and that that DNA is used to build proteins by providing specific instructions to cells. Because DNA instructions are the same across all cells, technologies based on DNA can be applied across all cell types. And because cells and molecules have specific tasks, specific products can be developed for these tasks, often with more reliability and predictability than conventional products. These two factors – the similarity of cells at the molecular level and the specificity of functions – together make a "biotech industry" possible.

Therein lies the promise of biotechnology and the basis for the "buzz" around biotech drugs. Today, understanding the genetic basis for disease – whether in plants, animals or humans – is paving the way for an ever widening scope of medicines that are highly specific and that can be tailored to the individual, giving hope and alleviating human suffering.

Biotech today

The biotechnology industry tripled in the 1990s and had a May 2002 market capitalization of $224 billion. In 2002, a total of 1,466 companies employed over 142,900 people in the U.S. alone. Of those companies, 318 are publicly held. Over 325 million people have benefited from the more than 130 FDA-approved drugs and vaccines produced by the industry. Over two-thirds of these drugs were approved in the last six years. A research-driven industry, U.S. biotech companies spent $16.3 billion on research and development (R&D) in 2002, with the top 5 spending an average of $89,400 per employee

Visit Vault at www.vault.com for insider company profiles, expert advice, career message boards, expert resume reviews, the Vault Job Board and more.

VAULT CAREER LIBRARY   7

in 2000. The scale of this effort has produced over 350 products and vaccines in clinical trials, which target over 200 diseases, including cancer, diabetes, multiple sclerosis, and AIDS.

Where is Biotech Applied?

Biotechnologies are applied across several sectors of economic activity, including healthcare, agriculture, food processing and industrial applications. The sheer breadth of these applications across the economy is important to take in and even more important when trying to plan a career. If most of your career is still ahead of you, you might well ask yourself two basic questions: "Do I like thinking about living things?" and "What sectors of the economy can I see myself operating in?" Being able to answer those questions early will go a long way toward choosing which biotech career path is best for you.

Here's a brief nutshell before we get into each sector. In healthcare, biotech companies have produced hundreds of medical diagnostic tests, including tests to detect the AIDS virus and home pregnancy tests. In agriculture, the industry has made more widely available foods such as papaya and soybeans and has produced hundreds of biopesticides and other agricultural compounds. Biotech products are also helping clean up the environment of hazardous waste and rendering industrial processes (e.g., chemicals, paper, textiles, etc.) cleaner and more energy efficient. Finally, the technique of DNA fingerprinting is making significant contributions in law enforcement and forensic science, in addition to anthropology and wildlife management.

Healthcare

Biotech products and techniques can be found in four major areas of healthcare, including: biopharmaceuticals, gene therapy, diagnostic testing and tissue replacement.

Therapeutic drugs and vaccines made using biotech techniques are referred to as "biopharmaceuticals," and are likely to become the leaders in the treatment of a plethora of disease conditions. Areas of active research include autoimmune disorders, cancer, cardiovascular diseases, genetic defects, infectious diseases, nephrology and neurological disorders. Specifically, biopharmaceuticals targeting anemia, cancer, heart disease, impotence, infectious diseases, lysosomal storage disorders, multiple sclerosis, psoriasis, and rheumatoid arthritis will likely be the most prevalent in the remainder of the decade.

Most biotech research in the development of pharmaceuticals is essentially a two-step process. Because the human proteome (the full complement of proteins in human beings) is composed of over 100,000 proteins, each with a specific function in the cell, biotech researchers first begin by identifying those proteins most likely to be responsible for the formation of a specific disease. Such a protein then becomes the "target." The field of endeavor that studies the human proteome is called "proteomics;" its goal is to understand the role of proteins in the formation of disease. Once a target has been identified, the second step can begin – the creation of therapeutic agents that can react with the protein to alter the pathway of a disease process. To date, some 500 targets have been identified, with almost 5,000 more possible by 2010.

Biotech products based on proteomics include protein-based drugs (administered by various modes of injection), such as monoclonal antibodies that may bind to cell surface receptors, and orally available small-molecule drugs (administered as a pill or capsule) that modulate cellular signaling.

A sister field to proteomics is "genomics," the study of the human genome – the full complement of genes in a human being. In addition to mapping genes, genomics seeks to determine their nucleic acid structures and understand their functions. Genes – like proteins – form a base from which additional targets can be identified. Gene therapy employs agents specifically directed against genetic targets.

Together, proteomics and genomics are reshaping the drug development landscape of the modern biopharmaceutical industry and rendering the process of creating therapeutic agents more precise, more efficient and more predictable.

Biotech techniques are also being applied in diagnostic testing. Among the tests currently available are monoclonal antibody-based tests, genetic probes, DNA amplification and agents to improve in vitro diagnostic imaging. Finally, biotechnology applications are being used to replace diseased or destroyed tissues. The technique is based on a substance called tissue plasminogen activator (TPA), made in the inner lining of blood vessels. TPA's main function is to prevent abnormal blood clotting.

Agriculture

With the world's population expected to reach 10 billion people by 2030, according to United Nations estimates, agricultural biotech is poised to make a major contribution to the enormous increase in food needed to feed

Visit Vault at **www.vault.com** for insider company profiles, expert advice,
career message boards, expert resume reviews, the Vault Job Board and more.

VAULT CAREER LIBRARY

9

humanity. Indeed, some estimates predict that the world's food supply will have to double to keep pace with this increase in population. Biotech based foods, biopesticides, and plant and veterinary disease diagnostics are some of the areas of application of biotechnology in agriculture. These products and methods are used to increase crop yields, decrease required input resources (e.g., water and fertilizer) and create environmentally friendly pest control methods.

Rather than rely on the traditional but more costly and inefficient methods of crossbreeding and hybridization, farmers now use biotechnology techniques to improve crop yields and enhance the quality of food products. These techniques are more precise and selective in that single genes with known and desired characteristics can now be moved to a plant, making the plant's growth characteristics much more predictable. In addition, depending on the gene inserted – often from a bacterium – the plant will also be hardier and more resistant to diseases and pests. In fact, transgenic or genetically modified varieties of soybeans, corn, cotton, canola, papaya, rice, tomatoes, potatoes, and grapes are already on supermarket shelves.

Based on microorganisms, biopesticides are toxic to targeted pests and are able to control pest populations that have developed resistance to standard chemical pesticides. One example is the Bt (bacillus thuringiensis) bacterium, which is lethal to the European corn borer, an insect responsible for $1.2 billion in crop damage in the U.S. annually. Biotechnology techniques are also being used to enhance the tolerance of plants to herbicides, which will kill the weeds that often grow alongside crop plants but don't harm the plant. This is useful because traditional sprayed herbicides are expensive, reduce crop yields and are not environmentally friendly.

Biotechnology has improved the nation's livestock by enhancing animal health and productivity. Cattle, pigs, and salmon are some examples of animals that have been genetically transformed. Within this decade, we can expect poultry that can produce eggs having lower cholesterol and cows that can produce lower-lactose milk.

Veterinary disease diagnostics help treat and prevent disease in animals. Improved quality of feed helps meet the dietary needs of livestock. Animals and plants are also being used as factories for producing pharmaceuticals and chemicals. The two immune system proteins, interferon and interleukin-2, are made naturally in cattle. Potatoes and bananas have been used to produce vaccines to treat a variety of diseases, including cholera, hepatitis B, and food poisoning bacteria. Such plant-based pharmaceuticals are much more cost-effective to produce and distribute than traditional counterparts. They can, therefore, become more widely available to both developed and developing countries.

Food processing

In the food processing industry, microbial starter cultures, enzymes and vitamins are being used to create food products that require fermentation, such as beer and cheese. More importantly, biotechnology techniques are being incorporated in food contamination test kits that help detect E. coli, a commonly found bacterium, and the Norwalk virus.

Industrial processing

Biotechnology techniques are also being applied to a wide variety of industrial processes, including: organic chemicals, energy production, mineral recovery, waste-stream reduction, bioremediation, enzymes, and bioelectronics.

In manufacturing and synthesis, conventional chemical engineering processes are giving way to technologies to create a variety of products. Enzymes are being used to convert cellulose to sugar, and from there, ethanol, an alternative fuel for transportation energy. Additional products from the conversion of cellulose include bulk, fine, and commodity chemicals and polymers. Bio-based products are carbon-neutral and, hence, do not contribute to global warming, are biodegradable, and make use of renewable resources, as opposed to fossil fuels. The benefits of this shift in manufacturing techniques include better economics (i.e., lower costs, higher profits), less pollution, and conservation of resources.

In other activity, genes in microbes are being modified to produce enzymes for underground injection to complete newly drilled oil wells. Bioprospecting refers to the search for microbes with unique profiles to be used in industrial processes. In the growing field of environmental biotechnology, the technique called "bioremediation" uses microbes and enzymes to clean up pollution.

Biotech factoid: After running aground in 1989, Exxon Corporation's Valdez oil tanker spilled tons of crude oil on the Alaskan coast. Bacteria capable of decomposing oil were used to clean up the oil that had penetrated rocks and gravel along the beach.

Biotechnology is being applied to the $400 billion forestry industry to increase its productivity. This is particularly important since global demand for wood products in 2010 is expected to be about 20% higher than the current usage of 1.9 billion cubic meters (source: U.N. Food and Agriculture Organization). Biotech processes are helping increase growth rates and render more efficient the conversion of solar power into wood production. In addition, biotech processes are helping produce trees that are healthier, more insect- and disease-resistant and less vulnerable to forest pests.

Enzymes produced by biotechnology provide the forestry industry with the means to pre-treat and soften wood chips, remove pine pitch from pulp, bleach pulp without chlorine, de-ink recycled paper, help convert wood processing waste to produce energy and remediate contaminated soils.

Industry Trends

Despite the downturn in stock price valuations since the spring of 2000, the outlook for the future of biotech is more hopeful than gloomy. According to an experienced venture capitalist, "Long term, the biotech industry is a growth industry and great to get into, since it is still relatively early in its evolution." But the industry is being impacted by several broad structural changes, technological transformation, demographic shifts and the emergence of new tools.

New focus on profitability drives company strategies

Perhaps the most significant change lies in the evolution of new business models for biotech entities. Although venture capital funding in 2002 exceeded that of 2001, the post-crash slump has forced a re-examination of how biotech companies are being kept alive as economic entities. From a focus on discovery research with decade-long horizons to bringing products to market and an emphasis on upstream technologies that will help identify targets from which drugs are synthesized, biotech industry business models have been evolving to product-centered strategies with shorter periods to return on invested capital. "We're seeing a shift from technology-based to product-based companies. Specifically, we're seeing a shift toward drugs as the driver of value, i.e., clinical compounds as opposed to technologies [genomics, high-throughput screening technology, etc.], which focused on the upstream processes of drug discovery. The time from the use of these technologies to getting a drug on the market is so long and that protracted time frame – 10+ years – limits what pharmaceutical companies and investors are willing to pay for them," a senior-level VC points out. "The focus instead is on nearer-term profits. Money invested in technologies has slowed down." This more pragmatic model is being implemented largely by creating a network of alliances between specialty biotech companies and larger pharmaceutical companies with established sales and marketing infrastructures.

Alliances and partnerships break down distinctions between biotech and pharmaceutical companies. Indeed, according to a leading academic and industry analyst, "the distinction is not so much between Big Pharma, and biotech, but rather between mass market and specialty pharmaceutical products." Big Biotech (the top 10 companies by revenues) have produced blockbuster drugs – drugs which have at least $1 billion in sales – and thus have similar characteristics of Big Pharma companies. In contrast, many biotech products are essentially specialty pharmaceuticals, with small highly targeted patient populations, that are often very expensive and marketed by specialized sales forces.

A scientific recruiter corroborates this perspective by saying, "In today's tough environment, VCs are looking to invest in more mature companies. They like companies that have already completed lead optimization and are now quickly moving in to process optimization. This means that they can, therefore, move into clinical trials fairly quickly, and as a result, the return on investment (ROI) will come faster."

The main effect of this shift is to create an environment where more companies become profitable. According to a senior director at a venture capital firm, "40 biotech and specialty pharma companies have reached profitability through 2002... [and] 30+ additional biotechs by 2006 will ignite investor enthusiasm" again. Furthermore, "an additional 96 companies have a scenario for profitability by 2006." Still, many other companies will continue to struggle and eventually be subsumed under the stronger firms. So despite some bright signs on the horizon, "as an industry, biotech will not become profitable for the foreseeable future. In the near term, it is unclear if that's going to change," according to a VC.

Mergers and consolidations

Structural changes are also having an impact. The number of publicly traded companies has declined through mergers and acquisitions, as the industry consolidates both within itself and across to pharmaceutical companies. In

2001, there were some 631 public biotech companies; in 2002 that number shifted downward to 613 public companies. The most significant mergers occurred within the industry: Amgen, Inc. acquired Immunex Corp., makers of rheumatoid arthritis treatment Enbrel, for approximately $17.8 billion; MedImmune, Inc. bought Aviron in January 2002, makers of FluMist influenza vaccine, for $1.6 billion; and in February 2002, Millennium Pharmaceuticals Inc. completed purchase of COR Therapeutics Inc., makers of Integrilin for acute coronary syndromes and patients undergoing percutaneous coronary intervention, for $1.8 billion. Analysts believe that this trend is likely to continue, as companies merge, restructure, or simply go out of business.

Globalization

The trend toward consolidation is also coupled with continued globalization of the industry, as companies seek out the best alliance partners from both domestic and foreign pharmaceutical companies, and as the latter gobble up biotech companies to expand their product portfolios. Increasingly, companies are listed on U.S. and foreign exchanges to expand investor bases. The explosion of Internet-based communication has facilitated scientific collaboration around the world. Finally, governments across the United Kingdom, European Union, Scandinavia, and Asia are increasingly cognizant of the need to invest in early-stage biotechnology companies as part of their economic development strategy. In the U.S. alone, funding for basic research for the National Institutes of Health has doubled to $23 billion since 1998.

The trend toward globalization has created a need to harmonize the global regulatory environment, as lack of consistency in patent and intellectual property protection has hampered the entry of Western companies and kept valuable biopharmaceuticals from reaching needed markets.

International investment in biotech has been and is expected to increase sharply throughout the decade, according to an industry report by Ernst & Young. In the next five years, biotech investments in India are expected to generate $5 billion in revenues and create 1 million jobs. Biotech employment in Japan is expected to grow from 70,000 today to approximately 1 million by the end of the decade. Biotech investment in China is expected to triple in the next several years to reach about $600 million relative to the 1996 to 2002 investment of $180 million. And in Singapore, the biomedical manufacturing industry is expected to reach $7 billion by 2005.

The United States leads the industry, generating some 70 percent of revenues and accounting for 70 percent of research and development (R&D) spending. The European industry accounts for 20 percent of revenues and 25 percent of R&D. This means that the most attractive R&D jobs will likely continue to be here in the U.S.

Within the context of these global trends, several additional forces are shaping the industry. The biotech industry is expected to grow at a rate in the high teens for the remainder of the decade, according to the Standard & Poor Industry Surveys. This anticipated growth is great news for young people considering a career in biotech or for more experienced professionals, who will find more opportunities. Growth will likely come from the major, more established biotech companies, since they have product sales, full pipelines, and stable fundamentals. In contrast, the smaller, emerging companies are likely to continue to struggle. S&P has identified several broad industry trends, which are fueling this expected growth in revenues.

Development of new biologic therapies continues apace

Development of new biologic therapies, particularly for the treatment of cancer, is likely to fuel the most significant growth in the coming years. With some 500 biotechnology-related drugs in clinical trials as of 2002 and some 400 agents targeted for cancer treatment alone, biotechnology is set to make a major mark in oncology. In 2001, Procrit, Epogen, Intron A, Neupogen, and Humulin reached $1 billion each in revenues and in 2002, Rituxan, Enbrel, and Remicade achieved the same benchmark.

In addition to cancer, the industry has ongoing research in many disease conditions exacerbated by aging, including autoimmune disorders, cardiovascular diseases, genetic defects, infectious diseases, nephrology, neurological disorders, lysosomal storage disorders, multiple sclerosis, psoriasis, and rheumatoid arthritis. The search for new biopharmaceuticals is important in finding cost efficiencies in the U.S. healthcare system, since biopharmaceutical drug therapy is less costly and less invasive than surgical alternatives and can be self-administered by the patient. As a result, the burden on the healthcare system is reduced via shorter stays in acute care facilities, such as hospitals, fewer doctor visits and less convalescent time in nursing homes.

Visit Vault at **www.vault.com** for insider company profiles, expert advice, career message boards, expert resume reviews, the Vault Job Board and more.

VAULT CAREER LIBRARY   15

An aging population means more favorable demographics for biopharmaceutical companies.

From a demographic perspective, of the 281 million people in the U.S. population today, approximately 62 million constitute the 45-to-64 year old age group – the Baby Boom generation. While the U.S. population is expected to increase 8 percent between 2001 and 2010, this cohort will expand by 26 percent over the same period and is by far the fastest growing segment of the overall population. In addition, with life expectancy in 1999 at 76.7 years and showing a steady positive trend, aging Baby Boomers are creating a rapidly growing market for aging related disease treatments based on biotechnology.

Furthermore, according to the Census Bureau, the over-65 year old population is expected to more than double between 2001 and 2030, which will represent 13 percent to over 21 percent of the overall population. Since senior citizens now account for approximately 33 percent of pharmaceutical consumption, their growing numbers can only bode well for the prospective demand for the industry's products.

Thus, by focusing its research on the four leading causes of death in the U.S. – heart disease, cancer, cerebro-vascular disease, and chronic lower respiratory disease – the biotech industry is set to bring to market biopharmaceuticals for which there is an expanding base of demand.

Information technology and bioinformatics is a transforming force.

Information technology is used in virtually all aspects of biotech research and development. Big players like IBM, Hitachi and other major IT companies are involved in activities ranging from computational biology research to biomolecular data management to biological modeling. A new field, bioinformatics, stands out as particularly promising in managing and interpreting the masses of data generated by genomic and proteomic research. Bioinformatics refers to the use of advanced databases and computer analysis tools to perform queries and simulations, cross-reference and compare data, archive test results, and collaborate. Because each biotech company needs a bioinformatics group, this new field has spawned academic programs and is one of the promising new career paths created by the industry. In addition, IT companies continue to spawn generations of supercomputers, drug discovery optimization software and physician practice management software.

Major Ethical Issues

Because it is grounded in the use of living organisms to produce drugs and food, the biotech industry has been grappling with ethical issues. The nascent industry proactively moved to regulate itself as early as the 1973, shortly after Drs. Herbert Boyer and Stanley Cohen successfully recombined DNA by forming the Recombinant DNA Advisory Committee (RAC) to explore the consequences of this achievement and to investigate the risks involved in conducting research in this area. During the next decade, as basic research moved toward product development, the industry again acted proactively by formulating and adopting safety standards for industrial manufacturing using organisms derived using recombinant DNA technology. Today, work on stem cells, cloning, and the development of genetically modified crops are the main sources of controversy.

Stem cell research

The stem cell controversy derives from the potential power of these undifferentiated embryonic cells to become differentiated into virtually any type of cell found in the human body. Scientists have the ability to maintain and focus the development of such cells to replace existing cells that are either cancerous or which have lost their capacity to function normally due to accidents and/or disease. Thus, in addition to cancer, patients suffering from diabetes, stroke, brain and spinal cord injuries, and diseases associated with aging can potentially have a new source of healthy cells. The consequences of successfully implementing this vision have raised enough questions that the NIH issued a policy in 2000 that would allow some research under strict federal oversight. In August 2001, the Bush administration restricted the policy somewhat but permitted continued federal funding. Subsequently, the NIH issued updated guidelines to the industry to implement the new policy.

Cloning

Cloning refers to the laboratory replication of genes, cells, or organisms from a single entity, meaning that exact copies of genes can be made. Although the National Bioethics Advisory Commission (NBAC), with industry agreement, has acknowledged the moral, ethical, and safety consequences of this activity, there is, nevertheless, one strand of cloning research that is supported by the industry.

Visit Vault at www.vault.com for insider company profiles, expert advice, career message boards, expert resume reviews, the Vault Job Board and more.

VAULT CAREER LIBRARY   17

Therapeutic cloning or somatic cell nuclear transfer (SCNT) refers to the use of undifferentiated cells that are genetically identical to those of a patient, and hence have no potential of incurring rejection. Such cells can develop into new tissues targeted to replace diseased tissues and offer promising new treatments for Alzheimer's, Parkinson's, heart disease, and many cancers.

Food and agriculture controversy with the European Union

Perhaps the most heated debate, however, surrounds the development and marketing of genetically altered crops. Agricultural scientists have long experimented to develop varieties of crops – among them soy, corn, cotton, etc. – that are hardier, more disease and pest resistant, and more nutritious. Success in this area has been remarkable: By 2002, a full 74 percent of the total U.S. soybean crop acreage, 71 percent of cotton, and 32 percent of corn used biotech breeding methods. Biotech has also produced fruits and vegetables (e.g., tomatoes and raspberries) that are longer lasting, less prone to disease, and have delayed ripening. Aquaculture has produced salmon and other fish that breed faster and cost less, and is more sustainable than fishing in the wild. Overall, the biotech food market is estimated to expand 18 percent to $5 billion by 2005.

Yet despite these advantages, concerns remain both at home and abroad. In July 2003, critics took to the streets in Sacramento, Calif., decrying the use of "terminator" genes and raising the possibility that cross-pollination of genetically altered foods with those grown in the wild will harm plant diversity and pose unknown health dangers to humans who consume them. Also in July 2003, the European Union (E.U.) ended the five-year moratorium on genetically altered crops it imposed in 1998 to have time to study health and safety concerns and to develop a system of tracing and labeling biotech foodstuffs. The E.U. requires such crops have clear labels. The U.S., along with Argentina and Canada, formally requested a panel of experts from the World Trade Organization (WTO) to rule the E.U. guidelines illegal. The U.S. and its allies claim that the guidelines are cumbersome, difficult to implement, and constitute a trade barrier. American farmers claim they lost some $300 million per year in lost corn exports. Furthermore, the U.S. wants full and unconditional acceptance of biotech-based foodstuffs.

Regulation of the Biotech Industry

Several agencies of the U.S. federal government regulate the activities and product introductions of the biotech industry; some have overlapping responsibility. The Food and Drug Administration (FDA) reviews and approves biotech products in the healthcare sector, much like it does for the pharmaceutical industry. The FDA approves the safety of all foods and new food ingredients. In addition, all producers are required to ensure the safety and quality of anything they introduce into the food supply.

Three major events are shaping the regulatory environment in the biotech healthcare arena. First, in reaction to criticism that it was acting too slowly, the FDA moved the review of biologic drugs from the Center for Biologics Evaluation and Research (CBER) to the Center for Drug Evaluation and Research (CDER) in September 2002, thus bringing the review of all human therapeutics under one roof. A major industry group, the Biotechnology Industry Organization (BIO), supported this move and expressed optimism that the review process will be expedited. Second, the appointment of Dr. Mark McClellan as the FDA's new commissioner in October 2002 filled a two-year vacancy, one which observers noted may have delayed approval of new products. And third, in August 2002, the FDA announced a new plan to improve the quality and safety of manufactured drugs.

Together, these actions will help stem and hopefully reverse the decline in approval of new products and shorten the timeframe needed for approval. According to the Pharmaceutical Research and Manufacturers of America (PhRMA), new product approvals have been declining from 53 in 1996 to 24 in 2001 and timeframes needed for approval grew from 11.7 months in 1998 to 16.4 months in 2001. In addition, New Drug Applications (NDAs) for New Molecular Entities (NMEs) declined from 43 in 1998 to only 14 in 2003.

Biotech factoid: Over 900 biotech products are currently in the pipelines, including over 100 products in late stages of testing.

In addition to rigorous testing, the FDA requires labeling of any food product produced from genetically altered sources, especially when the nutritional composition of the end product has been significantly affected. Any use of a known allergen must also be disclosed on the label.

The U.S. Department of Agriculture (USDA) regulates agricultural products produced by the food industry, setting standards to ensure that new crops created through biotechnology techniques are at least as safe and that pesticides and herbicides are at least as effective as those grown conventionally. Over 5,000 field trials have been conducted on over 20,000 plots in the U.S. since 1988.

The Environmental Protection Agency (EPA) oversees growing of plants with pest-protection characteristics and coordinates with the USDA and FDA, using its own statutes, and establishes allowable food residue tolerance levels for any new compounds.

Sources: Biotechnology Industry Organization; Standard & Poor's Biotech Industry Survey; Building Global Biobrands

Developing Products in Biotech

CHAPTER 2

Major Tools and Techniques

The biotech industry employs a host of tools and techniques to develop new drugs. Having a basic understanding of these will help you become oriented to how the industry obtains data and make you acquainted with the companies that specialize in these analytical tools. Although some of the minor players have been hit hard in the last two years, the major players – Applied BioSystems Group, Invitrogen Corp., Millipore Corp., and Waters Corp. – have introduced new products and continue to be profitable.

Tool/Technique	Description	Leading Company
Genomic databases	Databases that compile information on the characteristics, expression, and function of genes and proteins, the features of single nucleotide polymorphisms, aspects of medicinal chemistry, and drug screening.	Colera Genomics Group and Incyte Genomics Inc.
Biochip	Miniature slide or plate that allows researchers to perform tests to understand the structure and function of genes and proteins.	Affymetrix
High-performance liquid chromatography (HPLC)	HPLC provides a more automated way to separate proteins than do 2-D gels or isotope-coated affinity tags, but is not as sensitive as these methods.	Waters Corp. and Agilent Technologies
Isotope-coded affinity tags (ICAT)	A newer, more sensitive method for labeling proteins, ICAT can detect proteins that 2-D gels might miss.	Applied Biosystems Group
Mass spectrometry (MS)	Instruments that measure the mass-to-charge ratio of peptides (protein fragments) and allow scientists to quantify the characteristics of proteins.	Applied Biosystems, Waters, and Thermo Electron Corp.
2-D gels	Used to separate thousands of proteins from cell or tissue samples. After separation onto a gel, protein characteristics are analyzed by specialized computer software.	Amersham Biosciences

Visit Vault at www.vault.com for insider company profiles, expert advice, career message boards, expert resume reviews, the Vault Job Board and more.

VAULT CAREER LIBRARY 21

Tool/Technique	Description	Leading Company
X-ray crystallography	Used to determine the three-dimensional structure of a protein, as part of the search for small-molecule drugs targeting specific cellular pathways, which may interrupt a protein's synthesis.	Structural Genomix Inc. and Syrrx Inc.
Thermocycler or Polymerase chain reaction (PCR)	A machine that separates fragments of DNA samples. Among its many applications, PCR is used for paternity tests, to detect residues of transgenic crops in food and to detect viral diseases before symptoms are manifest.	Bio-Rad Laboratories, Inc.

What's the Difference Between "Biologics" and Conventional Pharmaceuticals?

Biologics or biotech products have several characteristics that distinguish them from regular pharmaceutical products. Most biotech products are proteins, which are much larger molecular structures than conventional medicines. In fact, industry insiders refer to them as "small molecules" to distinguish them from biotech products. Because of their size, most biologics need to be delivered into the human body by injection, whereas conventional drugs can be ingested in either pill or capsule form.

Biologics are also more expensive to manufacture, since they require special facilities where DNA can be produced and purified and where cell cultures can be cultivated without contamination. This is in contrast with conventional drugs, which are made or "synthesized" from inert chemicals and can be manufactured at a relatively low cost per unit. This makes biotech drugs some of the most expensive medicines available. Although a few biotech drugs are mass marketed and have achieved the status of "blockbuster" or at least $1 billion in sales, most are actually specialty pharmaceuticals with narrow, targeted, small patient populations. All of these characteristics impact the development and marketing of biotech drugs.

Recent Products

The U.S. Food and Drug Administration (FDA) has approved several exciting new products for market in the last few years. In May 2001, the FDA gave Novartis marketing approval for Gleevec, a cancer drug developed through rational drug design for treating patients with chronic myeloid leukemia (CML). In 2002, Gleevec gained approval for gastrointestinal stromal tumors, and may prove applicable to other forms of cancer. In May 2003, the FDA approved Gleevec for use in pediatric CML patients.

In October 2001, the FDA granted Gilead Sciences approval to market Viread for the treatment of HIV infection in patients being concurrently treated with other anti-retroviral agents and who were also showing signs of HIV-1 viral replication despite ongoing anti-retroviral therapy. Approval of this drug has been a boon for Gilead Sciences, whose second-quarter 2003 revenues significantly exceeded projections, due largely to sales of Viread.

In 2002, Amgen received FDA approval to market Aranesp for the treatment of anemia in patients with nonmyeloid malignancies, and where the anemia is caused by chemotherapy that is administered concomitantly. Aranesp also reduces the need for transfusions. Since its approval, it has eroded sales of Procrit, made by Johnson & Johnson. Amgen, the world's largest biotech company, hopes revenues from sales of Aranesp will help double its 2002 revenues, to $10 billion, by 2005.

In December 2002, as a result of its purchase of Immunex, Amgen also gained the right to market Enbrel, a billion-dollar drug for the treatment of rheumatoid arthritis, polyarticular-course juvenile rheumatoid arthritis, and psoriatic arthritis. By July 2003, the FDA's Arthritis Advisory Committee recommended Enbrel as the first biologic treatment for ankylosing spondylitis.

In 2003, Genzyme gained both the European Commission and FDA approval to market Aldurazyme, the first specific treatment for people suffering from mucopolysaccharidosis I (MPS I), a progressive, debilitating and life-threatening disease caused by an inherited deficiency of alpha-L-iduronidase, a lysosomal enzyme. This drug is the result of a collaborative effort by Genzyme and BioMarin.

In 2003, the FDA also approved Fabrazyme, an enzyme replacement therapy to treat patients with Fabry disease, a genetically inherited condition based on lysosomal storage disorders that has broad symptoms and can manifest in various degrees of severity. Fabrazyme is one of several new drugs whose

Visit Vault at **www.vault.com** for insider company profiles, expert advice, career message boards, expert resume reviews, the Vault Job Board and more.

VAULT CAREER LIBRARY

23

approval was fast-tracked by the FDA in response to calls for more expedient drug approval processes. An expensive drug, financing for Fabrazyme has recently been met with resistance from state-funded drug programs. In July 2003, the Health Department of Ireland refused to approve additional financing to make the drug available for its citizens, arguing that Fabrazyme could cost up to €200,000 per patient per year.

In March 2003, the FDA granted Roche Laboratories approval to market FUZEON, for the treatment of HIV-1, under an accelerated six-month priority review process. It is the first in a new class of drugs called "fusion inhibitors," which keep the HIV virus from getting into cells. FUZEON, combined with other anti-retroviral agents is indicated for patients already being treated for HIV-1 and who exhibit signs of HIV-1 replication despite ongoing anti-retroviral therapy. Roche Laboratories entered into a co-marketing agreement with Trimeris, Inc. to market FUZEON.

In June 2003, the FDA granted Genentech approval to market Xolair, the first humanized therapeutic antibody for asthma and the first approved therapy designed to target the IgE antibody, a key underlying cause of the symptoms of allergy-related asthma. Xolair is manufactured by Genentech and co-marketed by Genentech, Novartis Pharmaceuticals, and Tanox, Inc.

The story of Gleevec

Gleevec (imatinib mesylate) was developed through a strategy called rational drug design. This means that scientists approached the creation of this drug systematically by first identifying the gene and genetic defect that was responsible for CML, then creating a drug candidate that affects the cause of CML on a molecular level.

The first step – identifying the target – has been one of the more preferred strategies for discovery research in the 1990s. The idea is that, by identifying targets – specific sites on the cell plasma membrane or specific genes – that are the root cause of a disease state, researchers can create compounds that react with the target in such a way as to alter the disease condition. Thousands of compounds can be screened with modern high-throughput technology and computers can then help identify those compounds with the most attractive reaction profile. The main advantage of this strategy is that it increases the specificity with which a drug can be designed. The main drawback, however, is that it requires a long-term commitment of resources and is now considered too slow in producing results.

Rational drug design marked a significant advancement over the conventional means of discovering drugs – largely trial and error. Up until the advent of rational drug design – and advanced computing technology – drug discovery was a laborious, uncertain process with a very high failure rate. As late as the 1980s, for every 10,000 compounds synthesized by chemists in pharmaceutical R&D departments, only one made it to market! This is partly because targets on either cells or genes were not fully understood. Therefore, there was great uncertainty as to whether the thousands of compounds synthesized would have any biological effect. When a compound did show "biological activity" it also had to be subjected to rigorous testing to determine its safety, first in animals then humans plus its effectiveness or "efficacy." Rational drug design was one tool that made the odds more favorable. By the 1990s, of every 7,000-8,000 compounds synthesized, one made it to market. These odds may still not seem that much more favorable, but they represent a significant improvement.

Chronic myeloid leukemia occurs because the body generates a constant signal to produce abnormal white blood cells via this chain of events: a change in DNA which forms the defective Philadelphia (Ph) chromosome which, in turn, creates an abnormal protein that instructs the body to generate this constant signal. Scientists believe that Gleevec works by blocking this abnormal protein from telling the body to keep making more abnormal white blood cells. The abnormal protein is called BCR ABL tyrosine kinase. Unlike conventional chemotherapies, which kill all fast-growing normal and abnormal cells, Gleevec works by specifically blocking this protein. As a result, abnormal white blood cells are prevented from growing and their overall number is reduced.

It has been referred to as a "magic bullet" since it targets only the enzyme responsible for cancerous growth and leaves normal cells intact. This specificity factor is significant in that this treatment differentiates between normal and abnormal cells – a significant step forward relative to conventional cancer treatments.

The discovery of Gleevec – known in the scientific community as STI-571 – is credited to the persistent efforts of Dr. Brian Druker, who found that this compound blocked the enzyme that caused CML. Dr. Drucker and his team spent another five years creating a formulation that was safe and effective. The first clinical trial was a phenomenal success, with an astonishing 100% success rate. Success is based on the destruction of existing abnormal cells, reduction in the number of new abnormal cells and no serious side effects. In this case, Gleevec

Visit Vault at **www.vault.com** for insider company profiles, expert advice, career message boards, expert resume reviews, the Vault Job Board and more.

V/\ULT CAREER LIBRARY

25

turned out to have minimal side effects. Based on these results and the life-threatening nature of CML, the FDA speeded up the approval process. Gleevec was approved after only three years in clinical trials. This is an exceptionally fast approval since most drugs can take from five to 10 years to obtain FDA approval.

Although the market for Gleevec is small – up to 8,000 Americans are diagnosed with CML and about 2,300 die of CML annually – this drug is now available not only to the CML patient population but has gained approval for gastrointestinal cancer and pediatric patients. The story of Gleevec is compelling because it represents a more targeted therapy for treating cancer, it was made available through an expedited process, and has demonstrated the effectiveness of rational drug design.

The Drug Discovery, Testing, and Approval Process

Biotech drugs and conventional drugs get to market through the approval process discussed in detail below. Apart from that, as we've mentioned, the manufacture of biotech drugs is more complex and more expensive since special facilities are necessary.

Diagnostic testing devices or other types of medical devices generally go through a less rigorous approval process to get to market since humans do not ingest these products. Hence, the complex and expensive clinical trials are unnecessary and FDA approval times are generally shorter.

This next section is a broad overview of each phase of bringing a drug to market. Remember, that this is often a period of 10 to 15 years. This may seem like an eternity if you are still getting your education and are itching to make a contribution to the welfare of mankind. Many people spend their entire careers focused on one phase of the process, such as discovery research. Others become specialists in a single functional area, such as clinical research or business development. In reading through this book, continually ask yourself whether you might like the activities described and how well you might fit into the groups engaged in different types of work.

An overview of the process

The drug discovery, testing, and approval process in the U.S. is the most rigorous in the world, often taking years and hundreds of millions of dollars. The central goal is to provide the public with medications that are both safe and effective. The major steps in the process are the same for both regular and biopharmaceuticals and are listed below, followed by the average number of months required to obtain FDA approval. It's important to understand this process because it provides the framework around which all biopharmaceutical products are shepherded from the laboratory ultimately to the marketplace.

- Discovery
- Preclinical testing
- Phase I
- Phase II
- Phase III
- FDA Review and Approval
- Post-marketing Testing

The following diagram illustrates the drug development process for both regular and biopharmaceuticals.

Drug Development Stages

Discovery (2-10 years)

Preclinical testing (laboratory and animal testing)

Phase I (20-80 healthy volunteers used to determine safety and dosage)

Phase II (100-300 patient volunteers used to look for efficacy and side effects)

Phase III (1,000-5,000 patient volunteers used to monitor adverse reactions to long-term use)

FDA review/approval

Additional post-marketing testing

Years

0   5   9   13   16

Source: Standard & Poor's industry surveys

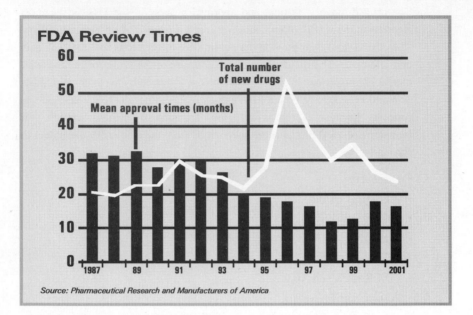

FDA Review Times

Source: Pharmaceutical Research and Manufacturers of America

Discovery

The biotech industry continues to be intensively focused on discovery research – the basic R&D from which potential product candidates are identified. The discovery phase can be broken down into several steps. Understanding how discovery research proceeds will provide you with a broader perspective, especially if you are considering a career in the laboratory.

Step	Description
Identify target	Focus is on identifying genes and their respective products, which are suspected to cause a specific disease. **Goal: Find and isolate potential areas for therapeutic intervention.**
Validate target	Once the target has been identified, its role in the disease must then be understood. Techniques such as differential gene expression, tissue distribution analysis, and protein pathway studies help verify a genetic target's role in disease formation. **Goal: Understand the target's role in disease**
Develop assay	A drug candidate screening process or "assay" is then developed to detect the activity that potential drug treatments have on the target molecule. An ideal assay is cost-effective, fast, accurate, easy to perform, quantitative, and amenable to automation. **Goal: Find a way to test a potential drug's effect on the target**

Step	Description
Conduct primary Screening	Compounds are then identified that have a minimum level of effect or activity against the target molecule. Drug developers then include these "hits" in subsequent screens. This step is often automated. **Goal: Find active drug candidates or "hits"**
Conduct secondary screening	Results from the primary screen are confirmed. In addition to its activity, the candidate drug's potency and selectivity are also determined. Drug developers then identify the candidate drug molecule with the most promising pharmacologic profile. Secondary screening is often done manually and is thus more costly than primary. **Goal: Find the most promising drug candidates**
Optimize leads	Once the most promising candidates have been identified, yet another screening step is made to identify the most promising candidate relative to safety and therapeutic efficacy. The products of these screens are incorporated in new libraries of compounds. This step can incorporate 10 or more iterations over previously screened groups. **Goal: Identify the drug candidates or "leads" with the best safety and therapeutic efficacy profiles.**

Preclinical testing

Step	Description
Preclinical studies	Leads are then submitted to a set of FDA-mandated animal tests before clinical trials on humans can begin. Animal testing is used to assess a lead's potential carcinogenicity and other toxicity. Other pharmacologic properties of the compound are also tested. The results of testing in this phase are incorporated in an Investigational New Drug Application (INDA), which is submitted to the FDA before human clinical testing commences. **Goal: Assess the drug's toxicity in animals**

Visit Vault at **www.vault.com** for insider company profiles, expert advice, career message boards, expert resume reviews, the Vault Job Board and more.

VAULT CAREER LIBRARY   29

Clinical testing

The results of the rigorous process of clinical testing are sobering. For each 20 drugs entering clinical testing:

- On average, 13 to 14 complete Phase I
- Of those, 9 complete Phase II
- One or two survive Phase III

This means that only 5 to 10 percent of candidate drugs submitted for clinical trials are approved for marketing, making the U.S. drug approval process the most restrictive in the world.

Step	Description
Phase I	The candidate drug is administered in small doses initially to a relatively small number of healthy people to test its safety. If proven successful, the dosage is slowly increased to determine the candidate drug's safety at higher levels. **Goal: Test the safety of the drug**
Phase II	The candidate drug is then administered to patients suffering from the disease the drug is intended to treat. Phase II tests seek to evaluate the drug's effectiveness and safety, includes a larger population of subjects and a longer test period than Phase I. **Goal: Test the efficacy of the drug**
Phase III	Testing here is the most complex and rigorous and often involves even larger groups of ill patients, who are monitored closely to determine the candidate drug's efficacy and identify adverse reactions. Tests are often double-blind and randomized with placebo control to remove the possibility of bias. **Goal: Verify the drug's safety, effectiveness, and optimum dosage regimens**

FDA review and approval

Step	Description
Filing of Biologics License Application (BLA) or New Drug Application (NDA)	The BLA and NDA are summaries of all aspects of a candidate drug's profile and intended use. They are compiled by the manufacturer and submitted to the FDA. BLAs and NDAs contain complete details on the molecular structure and formulation, the results of all phases of testing, production methods, labeling content, and intended patient use. BLAs and NDAs sometimes exceed 100,000 pages of text. Typically, the FDA requires 18 months to approve a drug after the manufacturer submits these documents.

Post-marketing testing

Step	Description
Additional indications	After introduction into the marketplace, the manufacturer often submits supplemental NDAs to obtain approval of a drug for other additional indications.
Post-launch monitoring	The FDA continues to monitor a drug after it enters the marketplace. If side effects show up when a drug is in wide use, the FDA may request an additional phase (Phase IV) of testing to determine the long-term effects of a drug.
Regulatory measures	The FDA may order a product recall if either the safety or efficacy of a drug is questioned. This can happen under several circumstances, including defective packaging, misleading labeling, failure to meet disintegration or content uniformity tests, loss of sterility, subpotency, or lack of evidence of effectiveness.

Visit Vault at www.vault.com for insider company profiles, expert advice, career message boards, expert resume reviews, the Vault Job Board and more.

VAULT CAREER LIBRARY   31

ON THE JOB

Biotech Company Organization

CHAPTER 3

Departments in a Biotech Company

Biotech companies focused on healthcare applications contain all the major departments of conventional pharmaceutical companies – R&D, operations, quality control, clinical research, business development and finance and administration. In fact, the top 10 biotech companies are essentially mid-cap pharmaceutical companies. Each department houses several functional groups, or specific, logically related areas of activity. The three charts that follow illustrate how departments and functional groups are organized in different size companies.

As you think about a career in the biotech industry, it is useful to identify the general area(s) where your primary interests and aptitudes lie. The organization charts that follow provide a general map of the terrain. Note that the charts build on one another, with more groups evolving as a company grows from a small organization (fewer than 50 people) to a medium-size organization (51-300 people) to a large organization (over 300 people). Before discussing the basic career paths, let's take a closer look at how functional groups are organized in different departments.

Research and development

The research and development (R&D) department is responsible for discovering promising drug candidates. The three major functions include discovery research, bioinformatics, and animal sciences. The discovery research function is responsible for performing experiments that identify either targets on the cell or potential drug candidates. The animal sciences function provides cell cultures, grows microorganisms, and manages the care of animals used in discovery research. The extensive data generated from experiments is analyzed with the assistance of the bioinformatics function, which assists discovery research in identifying the most biologically active compounds.

Operations

The operations department is responsible for making commercial quantities of a candidate drug available. Once a promising drug candidate has been identified, the process/product development function determines how to "scale up" quantities of a product to make enough available for clinical trials, since laboratory-size quantities are usually very small. When a product emerges from clinical trials successfully, the manufacturing and production function creates the final product – complete with packaging and labeling – that we see on pharmacy and drugstore shelves. Also housed under the operations umbrella is the environmental health and safety function, which assesses the environmental impact of a potential product.

Clinical research

Once a drug candidate emerges from R&D, the clinical research department takes over and becomes responsible for shepherding the drug through the FDA approval process. The clinical research function sets up and manages the clinical trials needed to determine a drug's safety and effectiveness or "efficacy." The regulatory affairs function ensures that all FDA reporting requirements are completed and submitted in a timely manner. Finally, the medical affairs/drug information function is responsible for overseeing all the information related to a drug candidate.

Quality

The quality department has groups focusing on quality control, quality assurance, and validation. These groups ensure that products are manufactured along rigorous, consistent standards of quality. This usually entails that well-defined and documented procedures are followed when producing a product either for clinical trials or as an end product.

Finance and administration

The finance and administration department contains these two functional areas as well as information systems and legal. All activities relating to the financial management of the company, its legal relationships to investors, creditors, and employees are housed in this department. The company-wide computer systems – separate from computing specifically directed at analyzing research data – are also managed here.

Business development

The business development group is typically responsible for identifying prospective new alliance partners and managing existing alliances. The marketing function studies markets, identifies target customer bases, and sets pricing and promotion strategy. The sales function actually meets with potential customers in the field – usually specialist physicians in targeted areas of specialization (e.g., cardiologists, endocrinologists, urologists, etc.)

Project management

Finally, many biotech companies also have a separate project management department, which is responsible for ensuring that work requiring the collaboration of several internal departments is discharged smoothly and efficiently This department oversees special projects that don't naturally fit into any of the traditional formal functions but that require cross-functional collaboration.

Company Organization Charts

As you can see from the charts on the following pages, there are many points of entry into the industry. There's room for a wide diversity of talent, personality types and temperaments. A good question to ask yourself is, "In what kind of environment do I feel most comfortable – a huge company with thousands of employees and a global presence or a small company where I might get to know virtually everyone by name?" This bit of self-insight will help you target your job search.

From the charts, note that biotech-related jobs utilize the talents of people in virtually every scientific discipline, as well as in the engineering fields and traditional business disciplines. For example, scientists specializing in any of the life sciences can find work in discovery research; engineers can focus on operations, manufacturing functions, or industrial processes. Medical and healthcare providers can work in clinical research or conduct clinical trials. Business-oriented people can work in business development, marketing, or sales.

Organization of Small Companies

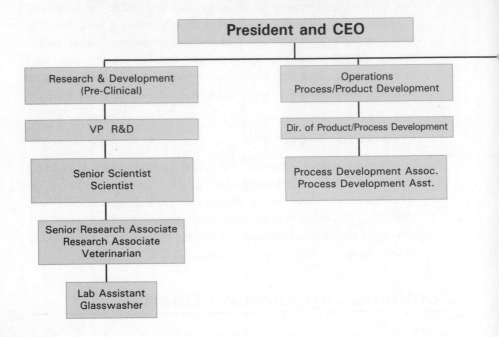

Depending on the size of the company, some of the departments discussed earlier may be either very small or non-existent. Most biotech companies are small, focused on discovery research and do not yet have products ready for commercialization. Therefore, they do not have either operations capability, such as process/product development and manufacturing, or the capacity to do clinical research. Their finance and administration functions are limited to a few people. Sales and marketing, as such, do not exist. If a research program is in the later stages, there will likely be a business development function mandated to look for alliances with larger partners, which can provide clinical trial, manufacturing, and sales and marketing infrastructure. Career tracks are either rudimentary or non-existent.

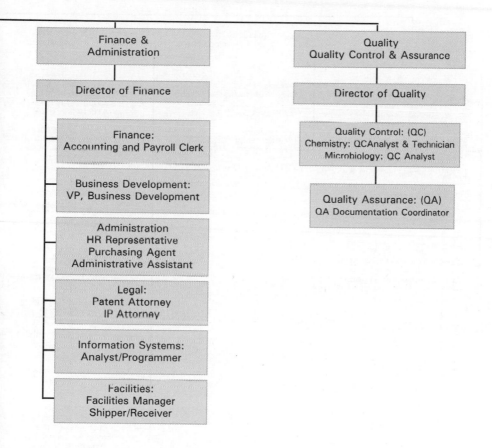

Visit Vault at **www.vault.com** for insider company profiles, expert advice,
career message boards, expert resume reviews, the Vault Job Board and more.

V/\ULT CAREER LIBRARY   **39**

Organization of Medium-Sized Companies

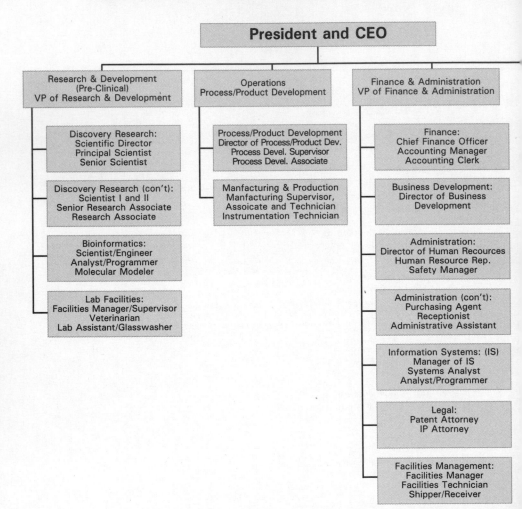

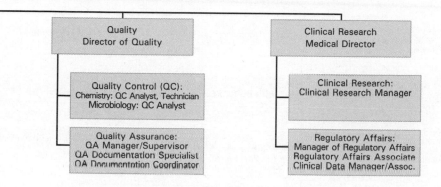

As a company grows from a small to a medium-sized firm, its R&D expands and its operations capacity begins to take form. Administrative functions needed to support these efforts also grow. Some companies elect to manage their own clinical trials. In those cases, the clinical research and regulatory affairs functions are put into place. At that point, the business development group aggressively seeks alliance partners to make manufacturing and marketing capability available. In medium-sized companies, career tracks are laid down and a hierarchy is formed in each group to give employees a sense of direction.

A handful of companies become fully developed across all departments and all functions. As we noted, the top 10 biotechs (by revenues) are essentially mid-cap pharmaceutical companies. Organizational structures continue to grow organically, functions are more fully differentiated and career tracks continue to become formalized, as more layers are added in each group. The human resources function in the finance and administration department becomes more fully realized and information services becomes bigger as more complex networks are needed. Business development becomes differentiated and occupies a role on a similar level as discovery research and operations. The clinical research functions are put into place as human clinical trials get underway and manufacturing capacity is added to the operations department.

Visit Vault at **www.vault.com** for insider company profiles, expert advice, career message boards, expert resume reviews, the Vault Job Board and more.

VAULT CAREER LIBRARY   41

Organization of Large Companies

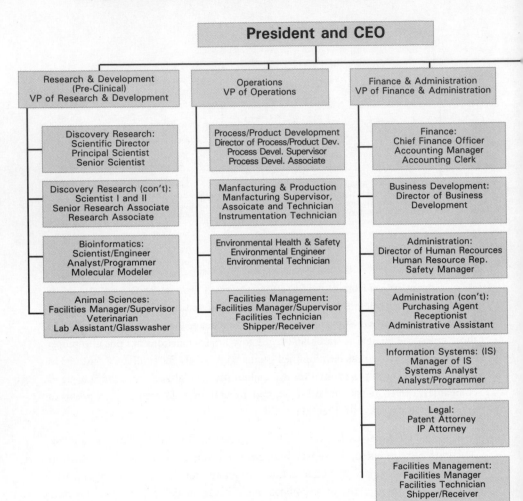

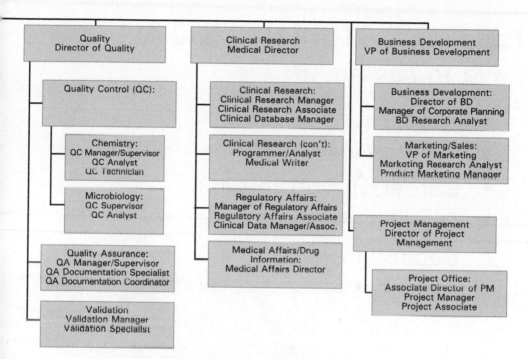

Source: Mass Biotech Council; Biotech Industry Organization

Visit Vault at **www.vault.com** for insider company profiles, expert advice,
career message boards, expert resume reviews, the Vault Job Board and more.

VAULT CAREER LIBRARY

43

Choosing a Career Path

CHAPTER 4

To Lab or Not To Lab?

Given the breadth of choices, you might well wonder how to focus your own career aspirations. You may be turned on by science while in college enough to earn a major in a scientific discipline but not be sure you want to make research your life-long career. That's fine, as long as you have a sense of how to manage the critical early years of professional experience. To help you get a wide-angle view of the major career paths available, we have found it helpful to think in terms of two fundamental paths: laboratory research oriented and non-laboratory research oriented. Within each path are several different career tracks, discussed later.

Laboratory research-oriented career paths are found in the research and development (R&D) department. This area is also called "discovery research" because the work involves discovering new processes, drugs and technologies. These careers involve "bench work," referring to a laboratory bench, where scientists set up experiments to generate data. In biotech research, two other areas – bioinformatics and animal sciences – are especially tightly integrated.

Non-research oriented career paths include everything else. Several functions – operations, manufacturing, and quality – have an engineering bent and are primarily focused on the applications of science. Others, like clinical research, include all the jobs needed to set up and manage clinical trials and oversee submissions to regulatory agencies. Note that the "clinical research" function includes all the jobs needed to set up and manage clinical trials. They are put here rather than in the research-oriented path since they require knowledge of medicine and occur in clinical settings – such as hospitals or clinics. Still others are business-oriented and include support functions, such as finance, administration, legal, IT, business development, and sales/marketing. Finally many companies have a project management function that helps coordinate projects that overlap among several internal functions.

The common denominator is that careers in most of these functions require at least an undergraduate foundation in a life science. This includes the more generic business functions. Many careers require advanced training in

Visit Vault at **www.vault.com** for insider company profiles, expert advice, career message boards, expert resume reviews, the Vault Job Board and more.

V/AULT CAREER LIBRARY 45

science in addition to education in a functional area. For example, attorneys specializing in intellectual property often also have a Ph.D. in a life science. Business development people typically have either a Bachelor's or a Master's in a scientific area in addition to an MBA. The industry sets these educational prerequisites for employment outside the lab because a thorough grounding in the vocabulary of genetics, an orientation to the basic concepts behind the products, and a familiarity with the issues and challenges facing the industry are necessary to get people effectively on the same page. The bottom line is this: If you are up and coming in the educational system, you are joining a limited pool of qualified talent competing for the available jobs. That's good news if most of your career is still ahead of you.

Laboratory Research Careers

Within a lab context, you can choose from three career paths: discovery research, bioinformatics, and animal sciences.

Discovery research

Since biotech is still in its infancy, most jobs in biotech companies, especially the smaller ones, are in discovery research. Discovery researchers can range from protein chemists to geneticists to biochemists to many other disciplines in the life sciences. There are jobs at all levels. With a Bachelor's, you can get an entry-level job as a research associate and work for several years, though you will need an advanced degree for more senior jobs. Most responsible positions, however, require a Ph.D. You can definitely break into the industry after undergraduate studies. Entry-level research positions will get your feet wet and give you a chance to experience the culture of research first-hand before committing yourself to advanced studies.

Animal science specialists

Instead of using chemicals the way traditional pharmaceutical chemists do, discovery research scientists use cells, which have to be obtained from animals, cultivated, separated, and utilized in special facilities. Discovery researchers rely on veterinarians and other animal science specialists. They grow cultures, make and purify DNA, and help conduct the earliest phases of testing, when a drug's safety is determined via animal testing.

Bioinformatics

Since nearly all experimental setups are computerized and reams of data are generated with each experiment, the results of biotech experiments are analyzed by specialists who straddle the fence between the biological sciences and information technology. These data analysts are called bioinformatics professionals and comprise some of the most sought-after employees in the industry. They help discovery researchers identify those molecular structures that have the most favorable response profile, and thus the most promising drug candidates.

Bioinformatics has three realms of activity: you can create databases to store and manage large biological data sets, you can develop algorithms and statistics to determine the relationships among the components of these datasets, or you can use these tools to either analyze or interpret biological data – e.g., DNA, RNA or protein sequences, protein structures, gene expression profiles, or biochemical pathways.

Choosing a Laboratory Career Path

So how do you choose which laboratory career path is right for you? To be happy and productive in your career, be sure to ask yourself some crucial questions.

If you're interested in a lab career, ask yourself:

Am I happier working alone or do I prefer to be part of a group?
The days of the lone scientist working in an isolated laboratory are essentially gone. Today, discovery research scientists work collaboratively both within their own groups and with other functions to identify potential new drugs. This requires closer coordination of projects and a greater emphasis on time management and communication skills.

Do I want to set up and run experiments or do I prefer to play with data on my computer all day?
If you like to fool around with instruments, handle petrie dishes with cell cultures, and mix chemicals, then a bioinformatics job may not appeal to you. On the other hand, if your idea of a fulfilling day is to spend 12 hours immersed in your laptop with a few breaks and an occasional e-mail, then a bench job will not likely be your cup of tea.

Visit Vault at www.vault.com for insider company profiles, expert advice, career message boards, expert resume reviews, the Vault Job Board and more.

VAULT CAREER LIBRARY   47

Am I squeamish about injecting animals with things that might hurt or kill them, or do I feel it's acceptable to do that if the purpose of my work is to help alleviate pain and suffering from disease in human beings? That's a really important question if you're considering doing anything in the animal sciences. If you can't come up with a clear answer, but are attracted to the life sciences, you might be more comfortable working with bacteria, microorganisms, or viruses. Handling living things on this level is quite different from working with warm-blooded mammals like mice. Remember, though, that any product – food or drug – that is ingested in humans has to be tested on animals and then humans before being approved by the FDA. There's no getting around this requirement, so even if you don't work with animals directly, you may have to read and think about the results of animal testing and later clinical trials on humans.

Non-Laboratory Research Career Paths

As discussed previously, non-laboratory research careers in biotech encompass a large range of functions, including engineering, careers in medical and clinical settings, administrative/support functions, and sales and marketing.

Engineering careers

Engineering careers have a strong practical application. Where discovery research scientists identify potential drug candidates, engineers are more concerned with figuring out first, how to ensure that enough material is available for clinical testing, and second, how to manufacture an approved drug. Engineering careers require a great capacity for precision, order, defined processes, and a need to see tangible results after a day's work. If you like your work to be exact and practical, engineering-related careers may be just the thing.

Four career paths exist in engineering: process/product development, manufacturing, environmental health and safety, and quality. The first three functions are usually grouped together under the operations department. Although engineering-related, the quality department is usually found as a separate function in the organization, regardless of its size, probably because its mandate requires independent judgment.

Process/product development

Process/product development engineers ensure that the first goal is achieved. They need to understand how a product's input ingredients behave when relatively larger quantities of the product are needed. It turns out that problems come up when scaling up quantities. Think of it as having to take your Grandma's favorite recipe for chocolate cake that comfortably serves eight and increasing it by an order of magnitude – now you need to make cake for 80. Chances are the mixer, pans and ovens used to make the eight-serving cake will not be able to handle the new cake. For that, you'll need industrial size equipment; you may have to adjust the oven temperature and time for baking; you may even need to substitute some ingredients that don't behave quite the same way. These are the types of adjustments process engineers need to explore to make larger batches of materials available for testing. Most entry-level positions require a Bachelor's degree and at least some industry exposure, which you can achieve with a well-placed internship or co-op program while still in college.

Manufacturing

Where process development careers have an investigative component, manufacturing careers are plant-based and focused on producing FDA-approved products for end consumers. Plant managers oversee this task through very strict standards of consistency and quality that have been codified and adopted industry wide. Among the many different types of tasks and procedures performed are fermentation, protein purification, solvent extraction, tissue culture, preparation of bulk solutions, non-critical aseptic fills of buffers, filling and labeling of vials under sterile and non-sterile conditions, large-scale bioreactor operations, critical small- or large-volume sterile fills and aseptic manipulation of cell cultures.

To qualify for jobs, even at the entry level, employers expect some familiarity with terms such as GMP, GLP, and cGMP (see Glossary). Manufacturing of biotech products requires expensive facilities because the end products are often proteins, which are bigger and harder to produce than the small molecules that make up conventional drugs. You must be able to run complex equipment and ensure that procedures are followed and standards are maintained throughout the manufacturing process.

Visit Vault at **www.vault.com** for insider company profiles, expert advice, career message boards, expert resume reviews, the Vault Job Board and more.

VAULT CAREER LIBRARY   49

Environmental health and safety

Fully developed companies also maintain an environmental health and safety group to assess the impact of a product on the environment and ensure that any toxic by-products of research or manufacturing are properly disposed. Environmental engineers test and monitor air and water quality, investigate the health effects of potential toxins, dispose of regular as well as hazardous wastes, develop procedures to control pollution and give input on how to manage the land around a facility. This task becomes especially important in industrial applications of biotechnology, where chemical spills can have devastating effects on the environment if they are not contained quickly. Keeping up and complying with environmental regulations also falls under this group. Environmental engineers prepare permit applications, perform regulatory reviews, inspect the operations at the company's facilities and participate in environmental audits.

Quality

Careers in the quality function focus on developing and implementing standards, methods, and procedures to inspect, test, and evaluate the precision, accuracy, efficacy and reliability of a company's products. These support tasks ensure that the company's submissions to the FDA as well as the products bought by consumers adhere to industry standards. In a tightly regulated industry with a significant potential for liability if a product is defective, careers in the quality function help ensure the safety of the consuming public.

Questions to Consider for Engineering Careers

Do I like abstract concepts or practical ideas?

The distinction can be somewhat subtle. You may be quite capable of handling abstract concepts but prefer seeing the practical results of your efforts. Discovery research scientists can spend years investigating potential treatments only to see their efforts fall short when a drug candidate fails in clinical trials. Engineers, on the other hand, can perfect a specific manufacturing process – say, the purification of proteins – and feel great satisfaction in seeing that single step fall into place. Where are you in this continuum?

Do I like to think in terms of how to make things step-by-step – in other words, about processes?

If so, then manufacturing careers will likely appeal to you, since much of manufacturing is developing process technologies and ensuring that those technologies are applied consistently. In practical terms, that means that you'll be making sure the millionth tablet of aspirin is the same as the first tablet or that the 100,000th protein that is used to treat a rare genetic disease is the same as the first.

Do I have a perfectionistic streak that insists on crossing every "t" and dotting every "i" in order to feel accomplished?

Perfectionists will find quality careers appealing. Your need to see procedures followed meticulously and to the letter ensures that their company's products are of the highest quality possible. That, in turn, helps ensure the consumer's safety as well as the company's profits. Think about it another way: Would you like a quality manager who does not have these traits?

Medical and clinical setting careers

When a product has been demonstrated to be safe in animals – that is, it's passed Phase 1 testing – it is ready to be tested on a small sample of humans and be submitted as a candidate for a new drug to the FDA. These activities occur in clinical settings, involve interpretation of massive amounts of clinical data, and require extensive documentation to the regulatory body. Two basic paths exist: clinical research and regulatory affairs. Jobs in these functions are usually grouped together in most companies.

Clinical research

First, let's clarify the term "research" in clinical research. Clinical researchers are physicians, nurses, and data management professionals who administer and interpret the reactions of patients who have been enrolled in clinical trials. Often, these patients suffer from the disease condition targeted and need to pass a set of qualification criteria set by physician specialists, who must ensure that their overall health status is sufficiently stable to participate in testing the drug candidate. Once a drug is administered to an enrolled patient, the latter is carefully monitored for reactions to the drug. These include desired effects and other "adverse" or undesired effects. Both sets of data are captured both manually and electronically. Sometimes, manual data has to be transferred to electronic form. All data eventually becomes housed in databases, where physicians and database managers

Visit Vault at **www.vault.com** for insider company profiles, expert advice, career message boards, expert resume reviews, the Vault Job Board and more.

VAULT CAREER LIBRARY

51

interpret the overall effects of the drug on the total population of patients enrolled in the study. These activities thus constitute research in a clinical setting using clinical data.

Medical knowledge at all levels is required for careers in clinical research – physicians identify prospective patients and interpret clinical data; nurses administer drug candidates and help monitor patient reactions; even database specialists need to have some understanding of the type of data the medical professionals generate in order to collaborate with physicians in interpreting it. With the hundreds of biotech drug candidates in the pipeline, clinical research jobs are expected to continue to be plentiful.

Regulatory affairs

Regulatory affairs is the other clinically oriented track. Jobs in this function involve dealing with all aspects of the regulatory environment surrounding drug approval, including submitting New Drug Applications (NDAs), preparing submissions to the FDA summarizing clinical trial results, keeping up with legislation affecting regulatory policy, ensuring the drug company meets new regulations, and working with the marketing function to make sure the message sent to consumers is consistent with federal compliance requirements. Careers in this function often require extensive reading and writing skills, as well as enthusiasm toward activities that protect both the company and the consuming public.

Questions to Consider for Medical and Clinical Setting Careers

Do I like working in a hospital or clinic environment, where professionals wear uniforms and sick people are treated?

For some people, that's a straightforward question. For the rest, think about how you might feel about going to a hospital or clinic setting each and every day and spending most of your waking hours there. Better yet, try it out through summer and part-time jobs, sample the atmosphere, then refocus your energies if you are not happy.

Does reading about how a drug affects humans or how a device is used on humans intrigue me?

If you come up with a "yes," clinical and regulatory jobs will give you ample opportunity to learn – in considerable depth – how a drug candidate affects the body or how a device is used to test for different diseases. Regulatory submissions to the FDA are often hundreds of pages long and require extensive staff to compile.

Do I like to think about the terms under which a drug becomes acceptable for marketing to the general public?

Keeping up with regulatory compliance requirements (making sure the company follows the rules!) needs people attracted to the law. You should also be fairly precise in the use of language, as different interpretations of legislation lead to different outcomes. The key is to want to communicate as fully and precisely as possible what the company's product does, how it works, and what its adverse or undesirable effects are.

Administrative and support function careers

Biotech companies have a myriad of other careers that support the R&D and clinical testing functions. Typically, the finance and administration department houses these career paths: finance, administration, information systems, legal, and facilities management. Although most companies have a separate project management function, the essence of this group is administrative and that's why we are including it here.

Finance

Although entry-level jobs in the finance function often don't require industry-specific experience, the more senior positions usually ask for exposure to the biopharmaceutical environment. Accounting positions fall into this function. Jobs are available at all levels, including analysts, managers, directors, and vice presidents. Increasingly, understanding how licensing deals work and how to initiate and implement mergers and acquisitions is essential for finance jobs in the biotech industry. Furthermore, leaders in finance play key roles in obtaining the financing needed to run the many small research-oriented biotech companies. To fulfill this mission, they need to have understanding of the company's core technology and be able to communicate its potential value to private equity investors and venture capital firms.

Administration

Administrative support includes administrative assistants, human resource professionals, safety managers, librarians, and external relations officers. In the larger firms, the latter comprise of public relations specialists, who deal

Visit Vault at **www.vault.com** for insider company profiles, expert advice,
career message boards, expert resume reviews, the Vault Job Board and more.

VAULT CAREER LIBRARY **53**

with the media; investor relations specialists, who deal with Wall Street investment houses and the financial press, and government relations specialists, who represent the company to government committees and stay abreast of important legislation. Since some aspects of biotech research remain controversial, the specialists in this last function play the special role of advocate for their companies.

Information systems

The information systems function is responsible for the company's computing and networking equipment, as opposed to the specialized equipment used by the bioinformatics group in discovery research. There are jobs for programmers, analysts, network specialists, cyber-security experts and web site developers and site maintenance personnel. As a company grows, it needs more sophisticated software to maintain its human resource function, in order to keep up with employee benefits, compensation, and training data. Working collaboratively with the HR manager, the IS department determines what hardware and software to acquire, installs it and ensures it is properly maintained.

Legal

You probably understand that biotech companies need lawyers to keep the company on the right side of the law. But if you think there's one generic biotech lawyer, think again. With alliances, partnerships, regulations (U.S. and international), patents, trademarks, labor laws, benefits plans, and mergers and acquisitions to keep up with, lawyers come in several varieties: patent/intellectual property (IP) attorneys, labor/employment law attorneys, and contract attorneys. Patent/intellectual property attorneys are entrusted with protecting the innovations generated by discovery researchers. The most important ingredient here is that the IP attorney "speak the same language" as researchers; thus, many companies require advanced science as well as legal education. Labor/employment law attorneys look after the company's human resources policies and ensure that hiring practices adhere to federal labor law. Contract attorneys help draft agreements that business development people enter into with alliance partners, participate in negotiations, and review terms of contracts involving the selling of the company or the acquisition of other companies.

Facilities management

In discussing facilities management jobs, first we should define what this means in biotech. In this context, they refer to the facility that houses the company – as opposed to the facilities housing animals used in experimentation. This career track requires some understanding of real estate, leases, zoning requirements, etc. as well as the specific needs of the company. Many companies need clean rooms and other areas in which to house special equipment. Nearly all need facilities that are wired to support powerful computing, networking, and other data transfer equipment.

Project management

While project management is more a function than a career path, it is possible to manage projects as a career. The key here is to be able to work with lots of different types of people, be very organized, and be able to push back to meet deadlines when necessary. Project managers make significant contributions when members of different functional groups need to come together around a task, usually geting a drug candidate into clinical trials or launching a product. It's not so much that functional specialists (scientists, marketers, regulators) are not cooperative; rather, each function has its own mandate and its own criteria for reward. A project manager can make a unique contribution by ensuring that each function has its say without tilting the company's resources (time, money, etc.) too much in any single direction.

Questions to Consider for Administrative and Support Function Careers

Am I a numbers person, at home with spreadsheets and concepts like present value, which other people find a little mysterious?

Answering "yes" to either part suggests you'll be comfortable in either an accounting or finance role.

Do I like to think about scientific concepts and like to understand what makes a discovery truly unique, but don't want to spend my life in a lab?

If this question reflects some of your inner queries and feels like you might be confused, think again. Patent attorneys spend their time figuring out exactly where an ingenious technology or process innovation can be patented. Their skills help protect a company's intellectual property, which is often the most valuable asset a small biotech company has.

Visit Vault at **www.vault.com** for insider company profiles, expert advice, career message boards, expert resume reviews, the Vault Job Board and more.

VAULT CAREER LIBRARY   **55**

Am I the quintessential "people person" – someone who wants to make sure people are treated well in the workplace and can grow in their careers?

Of course this sounds like human resources, but remember that HR is a cluster of functions – training, recruiting, benefits, compensation, and compliance – with some (e.g., training) having a primarily interactive component and others (e.g., compensation) dealing essentially with salary ranges, bonus structure, and other numerical parameters.

Sales and marketing careers

Career paths in this function include sales, marketing, new business development, and alliance management.

Sales and marketing careers in biotech are going through enormous changes, as a result of several factors: Differences in drug pricing across different geograpical areas are becoming increasingly important political issues; biotech drugs typically have smaller sales forces which have very high levels of product knowledge; marketing, at least in the U.S., is increasingly directed toward the consumer, as opposed to the physician; and consumers are clamoring for the government and insurers to pick up at least part of the cost of prescription drug costs. Beyond this complex web of economic forces, lies the business development function, which is itself composed of finding new business partners and managing existing alliances. Finding your way through this terrain is largely a matter of your skills set and preferences – where you experience satisfaction and where you get frustrated.

Questions to Consider For Sales and Marketing Careers

Do I like being part of a team, making complex information available to people who can help alleviate suffering and extend lives?

You may not think that this question applies to sales, but, in fact, biotech sales requires that you become an intrinsic part of a patient's case management team, working with physicians, nurses, clinical social workers, therapists, and other specialists to explain how a new drug works, what its indications are (that's what disease condition the drug is approved to treat), what types of patients will experience what range of adverse effects, etc.

Do I enjoy working with lots of business-oriented data, such as the number of patients a drug can treat, where they are distributed, how to reach them, what message to communicate so that they will consent to treatment, and how to ensure a company recoups its R&D investment as well as make a profit?

Those are essentially the tasks of marketing jobs. They are a step removed from the people focus that sales jobs have, but also permit you to see the bigger picture around bringing a drug to an entire consumer population. Marketing careers can be very quantitative and statistics driven, which may turn off some people; alternatively, they can be quite creative, particularly those areas that focus on creating effective advertising and promotion messages.

Am I a deal maker, with a secret longing to emulate Donald Trump?

As biotech and pharmaceuticals become increasingly integrated, new business development careers seek out attractive business partners. These careers involve understanding the product as well as the business and seeking out alliances that strengthen both parties.

Ok, so Mr. Trump is not exactly my hero. I like to connect with people, work things out, make sure things proceed smoothly.

If you're a people person with an analytical streak, then alliance management could give you career happiness. You'll be especially valuable since you will be the person who works out the inevitable issues that come up in any relationship. But you'll have to be equipped with enough knowledge of science to understand the product or service, enough business skills to sort out the most advantageous terms, and enough interpersonal skills to make sure both parties come away from the negotiating table feeling good about themselves and each other. While no one can guarantee career security in the modern world, we think that's an enviable skill set.

Visit Vault at **www.vault.com** for insider company profiles, expert advice, career message boards, expert resume reviews, the Vault Job Board and more.

VAULT CAREER LIBRARY   **57**

How it Comes Together

Developing and marketing a drug requires extensive collaboration between and among company functions, between corporate functions and external groups (i.e., government agencies), and increasingly, between corporate entities themselves (i.e., smaller research-oriented biotech companies and larger Big Pharma firms with manufacturing and marketing capability). For you to thrive in this industry, it is useful to become familiar with how people in different functions work together and where collaborative effort will be required.

Discovery researchers are primarily engaged in the focus of their research. As such, they tend to work together in groups, which are often organized hierarchically, with the most senior scientists also acquiring managerial responsibilities within the group. Except for the smallest startups, most companies have several groups of scientists, each pursuing different research objectives. Larger companies may also have several sets of groups dedicated to different therapeutic and diagnostic areas. Mid-level and senior scientists like to communicate with colleagues in other types of institutions, such as government-run laboratories (i.e., National Institutes of Health) and research centers in large universities. Thus, they attend symposia focused on their specialty areas to stay abreast of results obtained by colleagues outside the corporate world as well as to share their own results. Scientists also regularly share results in-house through company-sponsored meetings. Such forums, which permit the free and open exchange of ideas, have helped make the U.S. the leading center of global scientific research and development.

Group	Internal Interfaces	External Interfaces
Discovery research	• Scientists within own group • Scientists in other groups • Bioinformatics professionals	Scientists at government laboratories and university research centers
Product/process development	• Discovery scientists • Toxicologists • Clinical researchers	Clinical researchers
Animal testing	• Product/process development engineers • Quality and validation managers • Clinical data managers	Scientists at government laboratories and university research centers

Group	Internal Interfaces	External Interfaces
Clinical research	• Process/development engineers • Toxicologists • Clinical data managers	• Hospitals • Clinics • Patients • Patient advocate groups
Medical affairs	• Clinical researchers • Regulatory affairs managers	Regulatory agencies, mostly the FDA
Business development	• Senior executives • Medical director	Counterparts at prospective partner companies
Finance and administration	• CEO • VP, Business development • VP, Operations • VP, R&D	• Venture capitalists • Private equity investors • Investment press

With the help of bioinformatics and other database professionals, scientists identify the most promising drug candidate from the thousands that are screened. According to a bioinformatics manager, "We have very close relationships with bench-oriented scientists. We regularly sit together as a group to interpret the biological data and its statistical interpretation and usually develop a consensus understanding of what it means. Data is usually transferred from one group to the other over the computer network. In addition, the data is housed in databases for ease of cross-referencing."

The most promising leads must now be tested in both animals and humans. Product development engineers enter the picture and become responsible for producing the compound in sufficient quantities to meet the needs of animal and clinical trials. This means that the bench-scale quantities discovery researchers normally work with must be scaled up several orders of magnitude. Although conceptually straightforward, this task is often more complex than it appears on the surface, since some components of a formulation do not behave the same way in larger batches, special equipment becomes necessary to produce large volumes of compound, and purification methods need to be managed on a larger scale.

Product development managers need to ensure they meet the scheduling needs of animal and clinical trials managers, a critical step to moving the testing forward on time and on budget. The first step is always to test the product to assess the drug's toxicity in animals. Once they make the product available for animal testing, several groups work together to set up

Visit Vault at **www.vault.com** for insider company profiles, expert advice, career message boards, expert resume reviews, the Vault Job Board and more.

VAULT CAREER LIBRARY

59

experiments, collect data, and analyze it. These groups include the animal testing facility, quality, validation, toxicology, and data management groups.

A drug candidate that has passed the benchmark for safety then moves on to clinical trials in humans. Clinical researchers receive the scaled-up quantities of drug candidates to administer to patients in three phases of trials. Clinical research managers thus interact with product development managers to ensure steady flow of the test compound. Clinical researchers then administer the compound either in hospital settings or independent clinics under carefully controlled protocols. (A protocol is a detailed list of instructions on how to administer the drug candidate and perform the required documentation. Adherence to the protocol ensures consistency in administration of the test compound and validity of the results obtained.) Clinical researchers also monitor patients closely to record patient response. Clinical data then is sent to the clinical data management group for statistical analysis.

Clinical researchers interface with the regulatory affairs and medical affairs/drug information groups, who stay abreast of all regulatory requirements. These groups draft the various applications (INDs, NDAs, BLAs, etc.) required by the FDA, ensure that the company adheres to the rigorous standards required during clinical testing, and submit requests for expediting the process should the drug candidate be earmarked for a life-threatening disease. Recently, the FDA has made efforts to expedite drug approval. (See the discussion on biotech industry regulation in The Scoop section for such instances.)

As a drug candidate moves through Phase III trials – large-scale clinical trials where the optimal dosage is determined – and FDA approval becomes more likely, marketing groups enter the picture. At the larger biotech companies, the marketing and final distribution of an approved drug is implemented in-house. Most biotech companies, however, choose to partner with Big Pharma firms for help running clinical trials and for access to their manufacturing, marketing, and distribution infrastructures. Where this is the case, the senior business development people at biotech companies actively seek out potential marketing partners. Their focus becomes increasingly external, as they seek out partners with the best fit. Business development managers work internally with senior medical and scientific personnel on how to best position the product and senior executives to determine the optimal valuation of their offering. They then meet with counterparts at prospective partner companies to determine how to best introduce the product in the marketplace.

The Jobs in Lab Research

CHAPTER 5

Because the biotech industry is still in its infancy, most jobs are found in the R&D function. As products emerge from the clinical trials pipeline and become approved for manufacturing – typically a 10- to 15-year process – many new jobs in manufacturing, sales and marketing are likely to be created. In fact, according to the Mass Biotech Council, the number of manufacturing-related jobs is expected to increase sharply in the next few years, with over 1,000 new jobs in New England alone. This means that college students interested in a career in biotech manufacturing are facing good prospects for entry-level jobs.

Discovery Research Jobs

Research associate jobs usually have several tiers. After several years of experience, you can move up to a senior research associate. In this position, you will perform scientific experiments in collaboration with others and will be called upon to exercise your own judgment in completing experiments. You will also develop and implement tools and methods to meet the objectives of the research group. The highest level in this track is the principal research associate, who often acts as a primary investigator of independent research projects, where individual judgment is applied toward developing tools and techniques and interpreting results. Principal research associates may also have a supervisory role, as well as involvement in cross-functional teams. Increasing knowledge and understanding of FDA regulations is also expected as you move up the ranks. The salary range for the research associate track is from $40,000 to $70,000.

The scientist job is the senior researcher position in the R&D function. After several years as a scientist, you can expect to move to a senior scientist position. Senior scientists are recognized for their depth of expertise in their fields. In addition to conducting research programs, they investigate the feasibility of applying scientific principles and concepts to potential inventions, projects, and problems. Senior scientists also act as project leaders and consultants for the research function. At the head of each research group is a principal scientist, a scientist who is recognized as an expert and expected to have broad knowledge of state-of-the-art principles and theory. Principal scientists are also expected to help set the scientific direction of the company and make significant contributions to new research initiatives. Principal scientists initiate, direct, and execute research programs; develop advanced technologies; and test theories and concepts. They also participate in the patent application process, acting as spokespersons for their function as well as internal consultants to management in areas that impact implementation of research activities. The salary range for the scientist track is from $60,000 to $130,000.

Most scientist positions have at least some management responsibility, with the more senior scientists responsible for younger Ph.D.s as well as research associates. Most of the time, managerial responsibilities are limited to the group and laboratory level. Leadership positions beyond that usually require both management and scientific experience. Positions like a scientific director require over 10 years, and vice president positions over 15 years of scientific management experience. In all types of research jobs, knowledge of FDA laws and regulations is an additional asset.

In many of the larger companies, a scientific director, who reports to the vice president, shares the duties of leading the discovery research group. Typically, this position is more focused on managing operations. The director directs the work of several research groups, conducts planning, develops budgets, interfaces with managers in other functional areas, contributes to patent applications, and represents the R&D function in internal and external meetings.

The vice president of R&D is the highest-ranking position in the R&D function. The vice president sets strategic scientific objectives, develops operational plans, oversees the R&D organization, and assigns managerial responsibilities to each group. In addition, the VP provides leadership and direction on all research activities, initiation of new projects, and development of policies within a function. The vice president also represents the company in technical issues, initiates new technologies and processes, and manages scientific and technical career development of employees. The salary range for the scientific management track ranges from $100,000 up to $175,000 or higher.

Bioinformatics Jobs

Bioinformatics jobs come with several different areas of focus, which are less strictly hierarchical than discovery research jobs. The analyst/programmer job provides more focused computational analysis support. Analyst/programmers design and develop software, databases, and interfaces used to analyze and manipulate genomic databases. They collaborate with production to develop high-throughput data processing and analysis capability and to design and implement data queries, novel algorithms, and/or visualization techniques. Analyst/programmers also maintain large-scale DNA databases, prepare data for other scientists, monitor new data from public databases, and clean loaded data to satisfy quality control criteria.

The bioinformatics scientist/engineer job is one of biotech's hot new jobs. It requires expertise in any one of several basic scientific disciplines as well as knowledge of programming languages and databases. Scientist/engineers develop gene discovery algorithms for integrating sequence-based/functional knowledge about genes to help scientists analyze and interpret gene-expression data. They also analyze DNA information and identify opportunities for innovative solutions to analyze and manage biological data. In addition, they often assist in developing software and custom scripts to automate data retrieval, manipulation, and analysis; application of statistics; and visualization tools.

The molecular modeler job is focused on using computational techniques to help identify biologically active molecular structures. Molecular modelers support a company's discovery research by applying computational techniques to identify and optimize the number of hit/lead compounds. They also use their expertise in the molecular modeling of small molecules to contribute to rational drug design. Molecular modelers need a Ph.D. in chemistry, biochemistry, computational chemistry, medicinal chemistry, or a related field and at least five years of industrial experience, especially the molecular modeling of small molecules for rational drug design. Acquiring skills in commercial modeling software packages, database searching, docking and scoring functions, systems administration, and programming are recommended. The salary range for the bioinformatics track is from about $60,000 to $100,000.

Visit Vault at **www.vault.com** for insider company profiles, expert advice, career message boards, expert resume reviews, the Vault Job Board and more.

V∆ULT CAREER LIBRARY   **63**

Animal Sciences Jobs

As we've noted, the professional positions in animal sciences – those requiring a college and/or professional degree – are the veterinarian and facility manager jobs. The veterinarian job is focused on the care of laboratory animals used to test drug candidates in the R&D function. Vets (as they are often called) diagnose, treat, and monitor laboratory animals during the research stage of new drug therapies/discoveries. Vets observe and document animal behavior as well as oversee the testing and vaccination of animals. A veterinarian needs a doctor of veterinary medicine (DVM or VMD) degree; a license to practice; and several years of laboratory, veterinary, and/or animal experience in a biotechnology or clinical research environment. Veterinarians earn about $100,000 in a biotech firm.

The facility manager/supervisor is responsible for maintaining a stable lab environment, ensuring that equipment is functioning properly, that the lab stocks appropriate levels of all supplies, and that the environment is continually monitored. The manager is also responsible for processing requests for animals to be purchased and for allocating space, time, and resources for the company's animals. Many companies also prefer an AALAS certification at the technologist level. A facility manager/supervisor needs a BS in a biological science, several years of experience in animal husbandry and several more in a biopharmaceutical animal facility. The salary range for the facilities manager/supervisor job is from $60 to $80K.

Non-Lab Research Jobs

CHAPTER 6

Engineering Jobs

As previously noted, jobs span two separate core functions in biotech companies: operations and quality. Within operations are three groups: process/product development, manufacturing and production, and environmental health/safety. Within quality are the quality control/quality assurance and validation groups.

Opertalons

Process/product development group

In addition to the academic credentials we discussed previously, some experience with computerized instrumentation and micro measurement equipment will make you a more attractive candidate for an entry-level technician job. Expect to pull in between $30K and $45K. After a year or two of experience in the core tasks, as an associate, your responsibilities can include researching and implementing new methods to optimize a process. You can also be asked to assist in validating production processes. Associate salaries range from $35,000 to $65,000.

Most companies look for at least five years of experience before promoting someone to a supervisor job. Supervisors focus on managing the lab work involved in process development (e.g., scaling up formulas, fermentation or purification), so that laboratory scale quantities of product become available at pilot plant scale. Supervisors are responsible for developing new formulas, defining equipment specifications, and optimizing product yields. The more promising candidates also have specific experience in several types of processes. Supervisors earn from $50,000 to $85,000.

The head of the group is the director of product/process development, who is more focused on strategic planning and implementation as well as on tactical oversight of the group's activities. In the management part of the job, the director oversees production schedules, materials, equipment, and staffing needs; formulates budgets; represents the department on project teams; and attends business and technical meetings. In the technical part of the job, the director reviews supervisors' efforts at optimizing processes and maximizing

Visit Vault at **www.vault.com** for insider company profiles, expert advice, career message boards, expert resume reviews, the Vault Job Board and more.

VAULT CAREER LIBRARY   65

product yields and makes recommendations on new policies. The director needs a Ph.D. in chemistry, biochemical engineering, biochemistry, microbiology, or a related discipline and a good decade of experience that ideally includes experience with current good manufacturing practices (cGMPs), GLP, process development/scale-up, and methods/process validation. That usually goes up a few years for people at the master's level. The director job can bring in from $85,000 to $160,000.

Manufacturing and production group

The manufacturing group has a similar career path. Entry-level manufacturing technicians can expect to earn from $30K to $45K. You'll need several years of experience before being promoted to a manufacturing associate position, and along the way, be sure to understand purification systems, regulatory requirements and SOPs (standard operating procedures). At this level, you'll work under general guidance and be implementing new manufacturing technologies. Manufacturing associates can expect to perform tasks involving fermentation, protein purification, solvent extraction, tissue culture, preparation of bulk solutions, filling and labeling of vials under sterile and non-sterile conditions, large-scale bioreactor operations, and volume sterile fills. Manufacturing associates can expect to earn from $30,000 to $60,000

After several more years of experience, you can be promoted to a supervisor. Supervisors direct the work of technicians and associates. They are responsible for maintaining purification and production methods, processes and operations for new or existing products. They also implement and maintain production schedules and labor levels and ensure that cell culture and scale-up operations meet cGMPs. Supervisors have salaries ranging from $45,000 to $70,000

The next job up the ranks is as manufacturing manager, where the main responsibility is to oversee the work of several groups and set the goals and priorities of supervisors. Manufacturing managers have primary responsibility for compliance with GMP and other regulatory requirements. Manufacturing managers develop supervisors' goals and schedules, manage their activities and usually represent the manufacturing function at cross-functional internal meetings. You'll need at least five more years of experience to reach that status and can expect to earn from $60,000 to $95,000.

The top job in the group is the director of manufacturing, who oversees the development, implementation, and ongoing support of manufacturing business systems, including clinical and commercial production activities. At this level, the focus is more on ensuring that the facility is utilized efficiently and that a steady supply of product is made available to meet delivery schedules. Many companies prefer that the director have an MS degree and at least a decade of experience in biopharmaceutical manufacturing processes. Typical salaries range from $95,000 to $160,000.

Environmental health/safety group

Toxicologists design and manage the studies needed to determine the toxicological profile of drug candidates for both clinical trials and later product registration. They also interpret safety data and provide input on risk management programs. Toxicologists interpret and consult on safety data and provide direction and guidance for managing risk assessment programs. Toxicologists need an MS, Ph.D., MD or equivalent in toxicology, biological sciences, or other scientific field, and several years of experience. They should also understand both domestic and international regulations pertaining to toxicology. Toxicologists have typical salaries ranging from $70,000 to $140,000.

Environmental engineers deal with such environmental issues as waste disposal, pollution control, and hazardous waste. They help assess whether a company is complying with environmental regulations. Environmental engineers also prepare permit applications and perform environmental regulatory reviews. They need a BS in environmental, civil, or chemical engineering, or a related discipline, although many companies prefer an MS and several years of environmental engineering experience. They should also be comfortable with reporting and documentation and be familiar with compliance requirements for environmental regulations. Environmental engineers can expect to earn up to $70,000.

Larger companies will probably have several tiers for each of these jobs, especially if their staffing needs are large, but that is not usually the case. In most biotech companies, a few dedicated resources fill out this functional area sufficiently. If you are looking to move up the ranks in this area, consider either moving from smaller to larger companies or, alternatively, to companies that are primarily dedicated to this function.

VP of Operations

At the head of all groups in the operations function is the vice president of operations, who oversees pharmaceutical product development, technology transfer, and product manufacturing. This includes all the scale-up work and compliance with GMP and ISO 9000 specifications. The latter is a set of

Visit Vault at **www.vault.com** for insider company profiles, expert advice, career message boards, expert resume reviews, the Vault Job Board and more.

VAULT CAREER LIBRARY   **67**

manufacturing excellence standards. The VP is ultimately responsible for meeting FDA quality, safety, and regulatory requirements for new products. As with most senior management positions, VPs need a Ph.D. in engineering, chemistry, biochemical engineering, biochemistry, microbiology, or other related field and at least a decade of experience. This may seem remote if you're still working on a BS, but if you can imagine yourself leading the charge in a function where a Ph.D. is required, you'll do well to think about it sooner than later. Consistent with other management positions, most companies have a provision for otherwise qualified candidates without Ph.D.s, but that accommodation is more the exception than the rule. As an executive, you're in the big leagues now and can pull in base salaries starting from $150,000 and additional incentive compensation.

Quality

Quality control/quality assurance (QA/QC) group

Entry-level QA/QC analysts can expect to start at around $40,000. Companies that have senior positions are likely to pay up to $60,000. The two jobs are essentially the same, with senior analysts operating more autonomously. QA/QC documentation specialists maintain and implement the group's documentation system. Doc specialists ensure the accuracy and completeness of the system. You'll need several years of experience in a GMP documentation control setting to land one of these jobs. They tend to be parallel to the technician jobs, but require some experience to break in. Salaries range from $35,000 to $60,000.

QA/QC supervisors and managers have direct oversight of their groups and focus more on the hands-on development and implementation of standards and methods to evaluate the products being considered for commercialization. They ensure that products, processes, facilities, and systems conform to quality standards and FDA regulations, usually by conducting audits. Many companies prefer you have a Master's degree and at least a good half-dozen years of experience in documenting and implementing quality control systems. Typical salaries range from $50K to $90K.

Validation group

Validation specialists develop strategies and design studies to document that the product or process under study has indeed been validated. Their activities involve conducting qualification programs, writing protocols and reports, and providing general support. Typical salaries range from $45,000 to $85,000.

Validation managers oversee and review validation processes and procedures. They develop and implement protocols and test procedures to ensure that a company's products meet regulatory agency requirements, internal company standards, and industry current practices. Managers typically need a Master's degree and at least a half-dozen years of experience and can expect to earn between $70,000 and $115,000.

The director of quality oversees the work of both groups. At this level, the focus is more on meeting milestones and ensuring submissions to the FDA (e.g., New Drug Applications or NDAs) meet regulatory quality requirements. With patents already filed, this task becomes especially important, since American standards for quality are the most stringent in the world at this time. Companies want to ensure their submissions meet these standards since that contributes to minimizing time to market. Directors of quality typically need a Master's degree, preferably in chemistry and have a good decade of experience in laboratory management. Directors can expect to earn between $95,000 and $170,000.

Medical and Clinical Setting Jobs

Clinical research group

The clinical research associate (CRA) job usually has several levels and people can make significant contributions to the success of clinical trials. You'll be a stronger candidate if you are thoroughly familiar with FDA regulatory requirements. As we've noted before, CRA positions have several points of entry; what is required is a basic familiarity with the dispensing of drugs in a clinical setting. The salary range for CRAs is broad, ranging from $40,000 to $95,000, which reflects the several tiers in this career track.

Biostatisticians perform statistical analyses and programming for clinical trials. It is essential that they remain up to date in the latest information technology tools relating to data manipulation, statistical analysis, regression modeling, survival analysis, and analysis of categorical data. Adding knowledge of SAS and other programming languages will round out the needed technical skill set. But because they need to collaborate with MDs, biostatisticians should also have excellent communication skills. You'll go further if you can communicate the nuances of statistical certainty in the data (some would say, uncertainty) if you develop some people skills along the way. Typical salaries range from $55,000 to $115,000.

Visit Vault at **www.vault.com** for insider company profiles, expert advice, career message boards, expert resume reviews, the Vault Job Board and more.

VAULT CAREER LIBRARY   **69**

Clinical research managers are responsible for the work of CRAs and biostatisticians. They manage all aspects of the design, implementation, and monitoring of clinical trials, preparation of medical reports (e.g., New Drug Applications, or "NDAs" and Biological License Applications, or "BLAs"), case report forms, and informed consent forms. Managers also conduct site visits at each stage of clinical trials to ensure that investigators are adhering to good clinical practices (GCP) and address any issues that arise during the conduct of the actual trial. Clinical research managers typically need a BS/MS in a scientific or healthcare field and a good half-dozen years of clinical research experience. Their salaries range from $75,000 to $110,000.

Clinical data management group

The entry-level clinical data associate job usually has several tiers, with senior associates doing essentially the same tasks but with more autonomy. You can probably move up to an intermediate level after a year or two. Typical salaries range from $45,000 to $80,000. Many companies prefer that clinical data managers have Master's degrees to oversee the work of associates. Managers ensure the validity of clinical trials, design collection instruments, set up databases, prepare data for statistical analysis, and manage the flow of data to and from clinical trial sites. They need a half-dozen years of clinical data management experience and bring home salaries ranging from $65,000 to $105,000

As we noted, this group has other staff positions that contribute specialized skills. Programmer/analysts design and implement the applications that support clinical research and biostatistics. They play a leading role in analyzing, designing, and implementing client-server applications. Programmer/analysts create forms, menus, and reports based on functional and design specifications. The programmer/analyst is also focused on computer applications and implements design specifications according to the clinical information systems (CIS) standards. You can land a job without experience and move on to a senior position after a few years. Typical salaries range from $45,000 to $90,000.

A separate job is dedicated to managing the clinical database and has more of an IT focus than managing the collection of data. Clinical database managers are responsible for the information technology infrastructure that processes clinical data (i.e., client-server applications, such as Oracle, SQL, and GUI-based products). If these tech jobs sound appealing, try to do a few projects while still in school on clinical data or data that is relevant in the life sciences, since that intellectual orientation will be helpful on the job. You'll need a half-dozen years of experience for this lead role, and can expect to earn a salary ranging from $70,000 to $115,000.

Medical writers both prepare and manage the preparation of the many FDA-mandated reports and applications associated with developing a new drug. This includes setting up project teams, creating and supervising work flow processes, scheduling and tracking drafts, arranging for expert reviewers, establishing style guidelines, writing, editing, and physically producing regulatory reports. All positions require at least a BA/BS/MS. Senior level positions also need several years of scientific, medical, or technical publishing experience, as well as some exposure to FDA regulatory requirements for documentation. You would be surprised at the number of people with Ph.D.s in a biological field who decide they don't want either a lab job or a business job, and opt instead for medical writing jobs. You'll do well to keep this in mind, as such individuals have a definite competitive edge when dealing with the highly complex concepts of medical science. With the highest education credential, they'll also likely to have an edge in achieving the most senior positions inside corporations. Medical writer jobs often have several tiers and command salaries ranging from $40,000 to $105,000.

Regulatory affairs group

As with other entry-level clinical setting jobs, regulatory affairs associates can move up two or three tiers and attain significant responsibility after several years on the job. Expect to earn between $40K and $95K. In a related job, documentation associates/assistants coordinate the production of reports to the FDA. They maintain electronic files of drafts, reference collections and archives, and interface with project teams (i.e., writers, editors, etc.) to ensure timeliness of submissions. They also play a role in maintaining the software used to prepare the reports. You'll need at least a year of experience to get into this job and can expect to earn salaries similar to those of regulatory affairs associates.

Regulatory affairs managers supervise the work of both sets of associates and stay abreast of domestic and foreign registration requirements. They also prepare supplements and amendments to reports and monitor program costs. Managers need nearly a decade of experience and can expect to earn between $65,000 and $110,000.

Larger companies have another managerial tier, a regulatory affairs director, who plans and directs the group's activities. This involves interpreting policy, formulating strategies on how to best complete a submission and advising project teams. The director also interfaces with external parties in regulatory agencies to resolve issues and successfully shepherd a drug through the regulatory process. Many companies prefer the director to have a Ph.D. and at least a decade of experience. The regulatory affairs director can expect to earn between $90,000 and $160,000.

Medical affairs/drug information group

Many companies also have a separate medical affairs/drug information group headed by a medical affairs director, an MD usually with several years each of medical and biopharmaceutical or contract research experience. The medical affairs group is responsible for coordinating clinical trials. The medical affairs director oversees this effort and deals with groups that need medical information besides the FDA. Tasks include providing medical monitoring for ongoing clinical trials; communicating with investigators, sponsors, and clinical researchers; resolving medical issues; providing input for medical documents; supporting business development activities; and providing serious adverse event (SAE) consultation. The director also updates standard operating procedures (SOPs), ensures that quality and financial goals are met, and manages medical monitoring operations. A very senior position, the medical affairs director can expect to earn over $200,000.

At the head of all clinical setting groups is a medical director, who oversees all activities relating to clinical trials and regulatory agency submissions. This includes protocol design for Phases I-III, recruiting and managing of clinical investigators and data management personnel, ensuring compliance with good clinical practices (GCPs), and overall monitoring of clinical data as it comes in. The medical director also reviews results of Investigational New Drug (IND) studies and helps prepare New Drug Applications (NDAs) and Biological License Applications (BLAs). The director has a big role in creating and maintaining key strategic relationships (e.g., internal and external partners, clinical investigators, FDA regulators, etc.). The director is one of the most senior individuals in the company, usually has an MD/Ph.D. and six years or more of experience in clinical research management. The medical director has a major leadership role in seeing a drug through all three phases of clinical trials and ensuring that these efforts stay on track. People who earn both advanced degrees have a very high comfort level with academics coupled with sustained focus and a capacity to defer gratification. If that sounds like you, we wish you well throughout the long years of studying and test-taking and only recommend that you find a combined program so that you will have some youth left to enjoy after earning your credentials. One of the most senior people in a biotech company, the medical director can expect to earn a substantial salary, upward of $125,000.

Administrative and Support Function Jobs

This is the section where it's important to keep your perspective. Depending on the size of the company, the admin function can include a range of positions, such as finance chief, payroll clerk, HR representative, or IT support to make sure the computer network stays online. Other support functions, like legal, are frequently outsourced. In the larger companies, admin positions proliferate into a variety of separate functional groups populated by specially trained professionals. We're discussing all of them to give you a sense of the breadth of positions available beyond the entry level. In our discussion, we're also including two additional groups – project management and venture capital – since these roles are important in coordinating internal cross-functional operations and funding small companies, respectively.

Finance group

Larger companies will have an accounting group within the finance department. The accounting manager is in charge of the accounting group's activities, including completion of audits and analyses, compilation and reconciliation of the company's financial transactions, maintenance of the general ledger, and administration of the payroll. The accounting manager also oversees the cash inflow and outflow of the company, i.e., accounts payable, accounts receivable, cash receipts, etc. The accounting manager needs a half-dozen years of professional experience completing the processing of financial and accounting transactions. Typical salaries range from $55,000 to $120,000.

The director of finance is focused on managing the company's finance and accounting operations, specifically preparing financial statements, SEC quarterly and annual filings, and budgeting and forecasting reports. The director should have financial analysis and planning experience and be able to prepare financial statements and comply with SEC reporting requirements. The director of finance also assists in obtaining capital for the company, doing financial due diligence, providing financial analysis and research

Visit Vault at **www.vault.com** for insider company profiles, expert advice, career message boards, expert resume reviews, the Vault Job Board and more.

VAULT CAREER LIBRARY   73

support for deal structuring, and coordinating audits. The director can expect to bring home between $75,000 and $115,000.

In larger companies, the chief financial officer (CFO) manages the activities of the finance group. The CFO is in charge of all internal and external reporting, preparation of taxes, budgeting, planning, and analysis. The CFO advises the senior executive team on the financial impact of a company's activities and plays a key role in evaluating investments, purchases, potential alliances, financial obligations and contracts, changes in product line, capital spending, and sourcing/outsourcing options. Most companies expect you to have an MBA in finance for this role and experience in capital formation and mergers and acquisitions. The CFO should also have strong communication skills, since presenting the financial performance of the organization to various groups (e.g., employees, investors, bankers, boards of directors, and CEO) is an essential part of the job. A senior position, CFOs typically earn salaries ranging from $135,000 to $235,000.

External relations group

In the administration group, we're focusing on external relations positions, since these are professional level. You probably know that administrative assistant and receptionist jobs exist to support the executive staff, but these are considered para-professional jobs.

Several types of external relations roles exist to deal with different constituencies. Larger companies will have positions below the managerial rank. The public relations manager is the corporate spokesperson for the company and should be able to manage the development of newsletters and other publications. These tasks typically require understanding basic design, desktop publishing software, and editorial requirements. The public relations manager is responsible for preparing press releases, articles, and press kits; organizing press tours and promotional programs; and advising senior management on public relations strategies.

The investor relations manager is the liaison to the investment community, attending investor conferences and organizing analyst briefings. This person should understand the needs of the financial reporting community and be able to produce financial reports. The investor relations manager works with internal groups to articulate the company's value proposition and build the brand identity of the company's products. In smaller companies, the public and investor relations managers are often fused into one role.

The government relations manager is the liaison to the community at large and to government at all levels. A person filling this role should be familiar with the political process in general, knowledgeable of how political action committees work, comfortable working with government agencies, and planning fundraising and other special events. Other activities include introducing new programs that benefit the local community, serving as spokesperson and liaison to political action committees and key industry associations, tracking legislation that will affect the industry, and monitoring lobbying efforts. All of these roles require several years of experience and have similar salary ranges, starting from $85,000 and going to $100,000.

Human resources group

Even the relatively entry-level human resources representative job requires at least a year or two of experience to break in. HR reps do the hands-on administration of HR programs, and are involved in salary and benefits administration, recruitment and staffing, processing workers' compensation claims, training and development of employees, and implementation of employee relations programs. HR representatives also help implement government labor laws, including affirmative action, anti-discrimination, ADA, OSHA, FMLA, and wage and hour regulations. They can expect to earn from $40,000 to $60,000.

Larger companies will have HR managers who oversee the work of HR reps. Managers work on recruiting new staff (an important task in a growing company, developing training programs, defining jobs, and drafting performance review instruments. The next job on the career track is the director of human resources, who manages the HR function, including all staff, activities, policies, and procedures; identifies legal requirements and government reporting regulations affecting HR; directs the preparation of information requested for compliance; and acts as a primary contact with external resources (e.g., labor counsel, insurance brokers, and outside government agencies). You'll need a BA/BS in either business or a liberal arts discipline, although many employers prefer to see a graduate degree of some sort, and at least a decade of HR management experience, with special focus in organizational development, compensation, and employee relations. HR managers can earn from $60,000 to $110,000; the HR director can expect to earn from $110,000 to $130,000.

Visit Vault at **www.vault.com** for insider company profiles, expert advice, career message boards, expert resume reviews, the Vault Job Board and more.

VAULT CAREER LIBRARY   **75**

Information systems group

Analyst/programmers provide hands-on work in designing, developing, coding, testing, debugging, and documenting software applications. They act as IT consultants, technical support specialists, and technical trainers to the business units inside the organization. Analyst/programmers should be able to program in several languages (e.g., C/C++, Perl, SQL, HTML, and JAVA), be familiar with various operating systems environments (e.g. UNIX, Windows NT, Sybase, Oracle, etc.), have good diagnostic skills, and knowledge of relational databases. You'll need several years of experience to land an analyst/programmer job and can expect to bring home between $65,000 and $75,000.

Systems analysts focus on the design, customization, and implementation of software systems. They recommend new/alternative business processes and help develop a company's IT infrastructure by suggesting enhancements to existing software, developing new screens and functionalities, testing new systems, etc. Systems analysts also support existing applications. Systems analysts should demonstrate business systems analysis expertise and be able to implement packaged software. The better candidates will thoroughly understand the "systems development life cycle," have solid problem-solving skills, and be familiar with changing technologies. As with analyst/programmers, you'll need several years of experience to land a systems analyst job and can expect to earn between $70,000 and $85,000.

The manager of information systems manages a company's information technology (IT) resources – i.e., hardware, software, service, network, security, technical support, and user services. The manager also makes IT recommendations to senior management and helps develop a disaster recovery plan. Some companies prefer that the manager have an advanced degree to qualify for leading the group, but all managers should have a half-dozen years of MIS management experience and understand process modeling, reengineering, and systems analysis. IS managers can expect to bring home between $80,000 and $90,000.

Legal group

Larger companies have legal teams staffed by attorneys focused on different areas and with distinct types of experience. Often, these are some of the most highly educated professionals in the industry, as many companies prefer people with joint advanced degrees (JD and Ph.D.) for patent and intellectual property work.

Patent and intellectual property (IP) attorneys prepare and prosecute patent applications. Patent/IP attorneys work closely with scientists to develop the company's intellectual property, draft and negotiate license agreements for technology transfer, review contracts, and make recommendations on the company's intellectual property strategy. Prior to attaining a JD, you'll need a BS in a scientific or related field (note: Many companies prefer an advanced degree, preferably a Ph.D.), at least a decade of industry-specific experience in intellectual property and patent law, and admission to a state bar. Many employers also want experience in contracts and technology licensing.

Labor/employment law attorneys provide counsel for all matters involving human and labor relations. Labor/employment law attorneys work on employment discrimination, occupational safety and health, affirmative action, unemployment compensation, wage and hour regulation, wrongful discharge, etc. Labor attorneys also ensure that a company complies with federal and state employment and labor laws. In addition to a JD, you'll need a BS in business administration or a related field and several years of litigation experience in a law firm and/or corporate setting. To be a serious contender, you should also be thoroughly familiar with Title VII, ADA, FLSA, WARN, OSHA, FMLA, wrongful termination, discrimination claims, and traditional labor law.

Contract attorneys focus on preparing and modifying contracts, leases, non-standard agreements, etc. They need a BS in business administration or related field and several years of commercial litigation experience, as well as knowledge of contract regulatory law. Contract attorneys also review contracts initiated by other companies, evaluate risks, brief senior management on legal obligations and exposure to liabilities, and serve as agents on behalf of the company. All types of attorneys can expect to earn salaries ranging from $90K to $140K.

VP of finance and administration

At the head of all these groups is the vice pesident of finance and administration, who oversees all financial and administrative activities, policies, and practices of the company. The VP of finance and administration is also responsible for all other groups within this function, including finance, accounting, administration, legal, information systems, and external relationships (insurance, banking and lending). The VP plays a lead role in acquiring capital for the company, managing the execution of financial obligations (e.g., credit payments, collections, purchasing agreements, etc.) and maintaining relationships with financial institutions. The VP should have

Visit Vault at **www.vault.com** for insider company profiles, expert advice, career message boards, expert resume reviews, the Vault Job Board and more.

V∧ULT CAREER LIBRARY   **77**

experience at a senior management level, preferably in biopharmaceuticals. An executive-level position, the vice president of finance and administration can expect a compensation package that includes a salary ranging from $155,000 to $275,000.

Project Management

As we noted, biotech companies understand the need for internal coordination of projects that involve interactions among several functions. Thus, even relatively small companies have project management groups that have several types of positions. Project assistants provide support to the project managers and perform activities like collecting updates, maintaining documentation, and preparing status reports. To land a job as a project assistant, you'll need a BS in a scientific discipline and several years of industry experience. An administrative job within a single function is one way to get that early experience. If you go that route, make sure you seek out activities that give you some exposure to people in other functions and that require that you coordinate projects or events with other functions. As a project assistant, you can expect to earn from $50,000 to $70,000.

The experience requirement bumps up a few more years to land a job as a project manager. Here, you'll focus on managing all day-to-day activities, including developing schedules and budgets, leading teams, serving as intra-division liaison, communicating project information, staffing projects, reporting project status, developing resource-allocation plans, and identifying and tracking critical path/activities, risks, contingencies, and alternatives. Project managers can expect to earn salaries ranging from $70,000 to $90,000.

At the head of the group is a project director, who oversees all aspects of in-house projects, with special focus on managing teams across functions. Activities include developing and coordinating projects, contributing to the creation of strategic plans, developing internal management processes, identifying critical path issues and solutions, staffing teams and managing all phases of projects. A project director needs at least a BS/MS degree, although many companies prefer either a Ph.D. in a life science or an MBA in addition to nearly a decade of biopharmaceutical experience. People at the director level need to grasp the larger financial picture of the company, e.g., meeting revenue-generating milestones, have solid experience in managing cross-functional teams, and bring a thorough understanding of the drug

development process. They also have to deal with bigger potential conflicts.
Project directors can expect to earn from $110,000 to $145,000.

Sales and Marketing Jobs

Sales

Smaller companies focused on discovery research often do not have
marketing/sales groups. As companies grow and a product/service is refined
enough to commercialize, marketing/sales becomes differentiated from the
search and management of alliances. Biotech-focused sales positions have
the customary base and incentive structure usually found in sales jobs.
Salaries can start at around $45K and go up into the six figures. Bonuses are
based on meeting quarterly sales goals and can run into thousands of dollars
per quarter. Some companies have no caps on their bonuses. Other
companies offer stock options for their top performers. Nearly all companies
provide their best salespeople with special treats and perks, such as prizes and
vacations.

Marketing

The marketing function operates more traditionally. Marketing research
analysts can expect to bring home between $60,000 and $80,000. Larger
companies will have a senior analyst tier with the same responsibilities
operating more autonomously and at the higher end of the salary range.
Product marketing managers have overall responsibility for a product. The
product manager has a multitude of duties, including creating the marketing
strategy, defining the product's features and benefits, deciding on the
product's positioning, establishing pricing, planning the launch and post-
launch activities, managing the product's life cycle and providing high-level
sales support. Product managers also determine sales training and work with
either internal groups or external vendors to produce sales training programs.
You'll need several years of experience in market strategy, product
development and business case analysis to land one of these jobs, as well as
your MBA. The product manager job is like a mini-CEO, as you are
responsible for all aspects of bringing a product to market. These jobs tend
to be organized around specific therapeutic areas and often have several tiers
in the larger companies. Product managers can expect to earn from $80,000
to $110,000.

It is possible to move from the analyst track to the product manager track, but you don't necessarily have to do that to move up. Some people choose to remain market researchers and become highly skilled resources who provide marketing intelligence to product managers. You can also enter a product manager role without being an analyst, but you would need to demonstrate clear business credentials.

At the top is the vice president of marketing, who oversees development and implementation of strategic marketing programs, is responsible for overall brand performance and is accountable for optimizing return on investment (ROI) on marketing programs. Brand management responsibilities include defining the brand, implementing the brand campaign, monitoring its revenue and expense forecasts, and managing vendors and advertising agencies. To be a VP, you need several years of experience each in strategic marketing and marketing management with a focus in successful product launches, as well as your MBA. A VP of marketing can expect to bring home a salary between $110,000 to $150,000, along with other executive incentive compensation.

Business development

On the business development side, research analysts provide the extensive research and analysis needed to determine how and with whom a biotech company should partner with. Analysts generate the assessments that help business development management determine how to meet its goals. Analysts answer such questions as, "Should we expand organically or acquire other companies to grow?" and "Who should we partner with to become more competitive?" Research analysts work with attorneys to assess intellectual property and licensing issues, help develop and enforce agreements, and secure licenses for ongoing operations. Many companies have senior analyst positions with the same responsibilities, but operating more autonomously. Analysts can bring home salaries ranging from $90,000 to $110,000.

It's a significant step up to manager of corporate planning, a job that generally appears at the larger companies. They prepare long-range and strategic plans (usually several years out) and short-range/tactical plans (up to a year out). Other activities include designing and executing financial planning processes, setting targets, and planning guidelines. The manager of corporate planning works closely with the CFO to develop the company's financial plans for senior management, industry analysts, and investors. They complete competitive analysis and continually assess the prospects for the company. This senior position usually has salaries ranging from $110,000 to $120,000.

At the head of the group is the vice president of business development, a very important position in most biotech companies. The VP of biz dev oversees all efforts to identify, evaluate, and pursue potential strategic partners, joint ventures, and alliances. This person also directs the assessment of the licensing potential of targets, leads and drug candidates as well as the managing of all collaborations. They maintain partnership agreements and address the inevitable issues that arise in any relationship. Most companies ask for impressive credentials to reach this level: an MBA, a science degree and nearly a decade of experience that includes knowledge of due diligence, asset valuation, alliance integration, and portfolio management. As an executive, the VP can expect to earn a salary ranging from $160,000 to $190,000 and also receive additional incentive compensation.

Venture Capital

Although venture capital is an external function, we're including a few thoughts here to give you yet another career track that has played a huge role in building up the biotech industry. Venture capitalists (VCs) pool the capital from limited partners who sign partnership agreements, whereby they commit to making a stream of funds available over several years. VC firms identify prospective companies to invest in and structure rounds of financing from these pools. In biotech companies, the CEOs make presentations to VCs to secure financing; a VC representative usually sits on the company's board to ensure that the partners' funds are utilized wisely. In return for making their capital available, limited partners usually are promised an above average return – relative to the overall market.

The VC industry has evolved in recent years. "We're seeing an aggregation of capital in the hands of larger funds, with largest funds managing about $1 billion today, up from about $200 million just a few years ago. Consequently, more money can be invested in a company," says a VC. "Firms can now access $100 million or more from the VC market vs. only about $20 million a few years ago when fund sizes were smaller. This lengthens the time runway before they have to make a deal with pharma companies, and as a result they can drive better deals based on more clinical data, and consequently get bigger payments as well as get to keep more ownership of the drug. We're also seeing a growing up of the biotech industry, with the best companies having more resources at their disposal."

The few jobs available in venture capital are some of the most education-intensive of an industry noted for strong academic requirements. Associates

Visit Vault at **www.vault.com** for insider company profiles, expert advice, career message boards, expert resume reviews, the Vault Job Board and more.

VAULT CAREER LIBRARY   81

and more senior principals usually have an undergraduate degree in a scientific discipline. "Most firms are looking to fill gaps in existing skill sets (e.g., clinical, technology, finance expertise) but everyone needs to have some understanding of the science. Most people have at minimum – bachelors/masters degrees in either chemistry, biology, or other life sciences," says a senior-level VC. "In addition, most people also have an advanced degree or two: MBA, Ph.D., MD. Roughly half the people entering the industry at the associate level come in from business school and already have scientific education (often a Ph.D. and/or MD) and some industry experience."

Operational experience is also critical: "You also need to have several years of biotech/pharma industry experience. That could be from a variety of places – biotech, Big Pharma, management consulting, investment-banking, discovery research, etc. Most VC firms want significant operating experience." For someone who does not have that, "working in a senior management position in a biotech company" will help you advance. A second entry point is business development. "A potential alternative path with some similarities to biotech venture capital is business development at a biotech or Big Pharma company. These people sometimes also move into venture capital at a later date," adds the senior VC.

"There is no tried and true career path in the VC industry, largely because it's still a small industry. The top 50 firms control two-thirds of the capital on a global basis. The remaining couple of hundred firms invest the balance largely through occasional and/or smaller deals," according to a senior-level VC. "There are very few jobs and relatively few openings. People stay for several years in any one position; therefore, there may be 20 or 30 openings per year industry-wide." Typical salaries range from $80,000 to $250,000 or more, including bonuses.

A senior VC gives this advice for people wishing to enter the industry: "Know the industry. I can't emphasize that enough since decisions are not made in a vacuum. You need to know what's going on in the industry worldwide – the major trends, the economics of drug development, the latest deals and products coming to market, etc. You also need to have a network to evaluate opportunities and staff senior positions."

Profiles of Biotech Professionals

CHAPTER 7

Entry-Level Scientist

Scientists typically work in discovery research. At the entry level, senior researchers will supervise your work closely and you will spend most days interacting with other members of your work group. Your supervisor will set goals and provide guidance on how to best meet them. Entry-level positions, such as the one described below, are a great way to get a first-hand feel for what the lifestyle of a scientific career feels like, as you will be able to observe the work and demands made on more senior people, as well as experience the pace and rhythm of research yourself.

Name of position	Assistant Scientist
Function	Discovery Research
Education level	BS, Solid State Chemistry and Materials Engineering
Company type and size	100 employees; small, private specialty pharmaceuticals company
Hours per week	40-45 hours
Salary range	$40,000 – $60,000
Perks	Stock options, subsidized breakfast and lunch for small fee

What are your responsibilities?

In my job, I investigate the solid form of a compound or active pharmaceutical ingredient (API) to see the way its molecules are arranged. Ibuprophen and acetaminophen are two such APIs. The compounds come from Big Pharma companies we collaborate with and are usually in the pre-clinical stage of development. We use both high-throughput technology (100-1,000 analyses for a given compound using information technology) as well as bench-top chemistry to run our investigations. We typically run several screens – e.g., Polymorph screens, salt screens, and crystallization screens.

We are basically looking to find all solid forms of a compound, since different forms have different properties – e.g., stability, bioavailability, solubility, etc. High-throughput analyses help us determine the optimal set of properties for a drug candidate. Sometimes, we are looking for a particular set of properties. Other times, we are just exploring to see how the compound behaves.

I help execute experiments, gather and analyze data, present findings to either my supervisor or at formal meetings, write reports, keep lab notebooks, and make presentations to my group.

What are the criteria for success in this position?

You need ability to work with minimal guidance, to know when to present findings and to ask for advice at key points in a project. Good communication skills are critical. Since I only talk to my supervisor for 10 minutes a day, it's important to address issues and get enough guidance to go forward with my experiments for the day. Time management skills are required to handle the workload.

What advice do you have for job seekers?

See if your college will let you work in the industry instead of doing a senior thesis. Also, seek out professors who might have contacts in the industry.

A Day in the Life: Entry-Level Scientist

8:15 a.m.: I come in and check my e-mail, then plan the day. I usually have to communicate with the operations group (they run the high-throughput screens) to check on the status of ongoing experiments so I can go from primary to secondary characterizations.

9:15 a.m.: I go to the lab after about an hour to check on samples left overnight (for example, to see if a drug crystallized), characterize samples from the previous afternoon to integrate the data collected the previous day, and characterize new samples that have come in that day.

12:00 p.m.: The company runs presentations during lunch, where we learn what else is going on both within the company and with the Big Pharma companies who supply us with compounds. Speakers might be a group member from a different group giving an update, a patent lawyer briefing us on legal issues in patent protection, or a member of the products group describing ongoing product development work.

1:00 p.m.: Do data analysis at my desk (e.g., powder x-ray diffraction, differential scanning calorimetry, thermal gravimetric analysis).

3:00 p.m.: Go to group meeting (my group has six members) to update our supervisor on the status of projects, either independent projects or larger projects that have several team members. The supervisor will ask questions and give advice on running further experiments or recommending additional data points to be collected. The supervisor also gives us a heads up on what compounds are coming in during the next few weeks. This gives us an idea of the workload in the group.

4:00 p.m.: Update lab notebook with either data collected that day or experiments started. Get started on experiments that can be set up and run overnight.

5:00 p.m.: Prepare for weekly meetings with the entire solid state chemistry group (15 members). Typically, I make a PowerPoint presentation using tables and charts of data, a summary, and discussion points.

5:30 p.m.: Commute home

Assistant Scientist Uppers and Downers

Uppers

I like having a variety of tasks, gathering data through multiple methods, and trying to interpret data from both high-throughput experiments as well as from bench-top experiments.I like the sense of contributing to understanding drug candidates that are likely to get into clinical trials. I like being exposed to industry and to the various issues in the pharmaceutical industry, both within my field and outside – largely from presentations – from the senior scientists and other experts.

Downers

I sometimes have tedious tasks, such as weighing out lots of samples from high-throughput experiments or doing the same technique on many samples. Sometimes, I feel limited by having only a BS degree since so many people have Ph.D.s and have more in their heads to work with. That creates a great desire to go on to earning an advanced degree and to making a bigger contribution.

Visit Vault at **www.vault.com** for insider company profiles, expert advice,
career message boards, expert resume reviews, the Vault Job Board and more.

V/\ULT CAREER LIBRARY   **85**

Manufacturing/Operations Manager

The manufacturing/operations function houses the engineers needed to develop the processes required to produce enough compound for clinical trials. The senior manager's role described below illustrates the scope of responsibilities expected to fulfill this goal. Note that, unlike discovery research roles, people's work in the operations function is more time limited, and it becomes more important to meet externally defined deadlines – i.e., produce compounds according to the needs of the clinical trials timetables.

Name of position	Director of Process Development
Function	Manufacturing; Supervise 8-10 technical staff, including 2 Ph.D.s
Education level	Ph.D., Chemical Engineering
Company type and size	240 employees; mid-size company; $30 million in revenue
Hours per week	50
Salary range	$110,000 – $150,000
Perks	15 percent performance bonus, stock options

What are your responsibilities?

I get the opportunity to work with cells in a position with key responsibility for moving a product into clinical trials. The essence of my job is troubleshooting to see what doesn't work. My job has two goals:

• Take product concepts from research to manufacturing: scale ups and SOP (standard operating procedures) writing.

• Manufacturing of a candidate product for use in a Phase I or II clinical trial.

What are the criteria for success in this position?

You need a good sense of both engineering and biology. In addition, a successful person in this job will have a persistent optimism, good communication skills, salesmanship (to justify resources on a project), the ability to motivate people, a vision as to where the projects need to go, time management skills, a good sense of priorities, and a good network to keep current on new process engineering ideas.

What advice do you have for job seekers?

Develop or demonstrate clear successes at scaling up processes that shows a solid understanding of both the biological and engineering aspects. In addition, some understanding of good manufacturing processes (GMPs) and some interaction with the FDA are helpful. Above all, good people management skills are essential.

A Day in the Life: Manufacturing/Operations Manager

8:00 a.m.: Check in with people in the lab; review tasks for the day to understand what issues are on the table. Typical tasks include:·

- Track which experiments are running (e.g., effect of cell number density).
- Check possible presence of cell contamination· Monitor adequacy of supplies.
- Align schedules across cross-functional tasks (e.g., biochemical analyses conducted by other departments).

9:00 a.m.: Have a weekly two-hour meeting to review general project status. We go over:

- Whether the experiments we ran gave the results expected? (e.g., what was the effect of cell temperature?)
- Depending on results, we hold discussions with other departments to develop methods needed to complete our experiments (e.g., flow cytometry)
- Determine if we are on track to meet the timetable set by program management.

11:00 a.m.: Meet with one or both senior direct reports (Ph.D.s) to review the progress of their research, which involves:

- Developing new immunomagnetic separation schemes to harvest desirable kinds of immune cells.
- Modifying and optimizing a procedure for encouraging pancreatic stem cells to grow.
- Developing assays to estimate degree of cellular differentiation.

12:00 p.m.: Check in with BS/MS direct reports and redirect resources, as needed. This requires that I assign specific laboratory tasks to different people based on overall work load and skill sets [e.g., who is going to do cell culture, HPLC (high pressure liquid chromatography) analysis, or who is going to stock the lab].

1:00 p.m.: Meet with program management or IT to discuss ongoing data programs. This requires that I determine where we have to support other projects for different departments or different directors as well as

Visit Vault at **www.vault.com** for insider company profiles, expert advice, career message boards, expert resume reviews, the Vault Job Board and more.

VAULT CAREER LIBRARY   87

review ongoing work with IT to establish a lab information management (LIMs) system.

2:00 p.m.: Attend a cross-functional meeting with representatives of other departments to coordinate scheduling and resource allocation of the group, ensure that the work load was properly staffed, and that work moved from one department to another smoothly (e.g., flow cytometry sample number, time of delivery, and overall through-put).

3:00 p.m.: Meet with my entire group for presentation of data, general administrative issues, announcements, and goal-sharing among direct reports. Agenda topics include:

- New hires, procedures, or upcoming meetings.
- Handout summaries of recent results (including graphs, charts, and bullet points).
- Review of experimental results, including cell growth curves, cell characterizations, and inventory levels of biological materials used in cell research.

4:00 p.m.: Catch up on e-mail, approve orders, do paperwork, check inventory, talk with purchasing or quality about ongoing issues, including talking about quality issues, tests out of specifications, new SOPs, or changes in SOPs

5:00 p.m.: Meet with clinical trials staff to discuss timelines and overall preparedness for clinical trials (e.g., did we have the cells to treat the patients?)

6:00 p.m.: Commute home

8:00 p.m.: Read journal articles and keep up with literature (e.g., *Experimental Hematology*, *Blood*). Prepare for presentations either to senior management or general group (e.g., data review, results of current experiments, plans for future experiments)

Process Development Uppers and Downers

Uppers

I like seeing the results of scaling up – being able to make quantities needed to do clinical trials. I like to understand what can scale directly and to solve the challenges of what cannot be scaled. It's like having a favorite chocolate cake recipe that you make for six but now you need to make it for 1,000. I find out what ingredients have to be substituted, what containers are needed to handle the larger-size batches, and what type of oven gives the best results.

Downers

I get frustrated when the troubleshooting doesn't work, when we have trouble figuring out what we need to do differently. Also, communication with senior management to meet deadlines can be challenging and managing expectations about what can be done becomes important. Many frustrations are things that have nothing to do with science.

Business Development Manager

The business development role has emerged in the biotech industry to help generate revenue from existing technology, to extend the venture capital investment that funds discovery research. People often enter the function as business analysts, researching prospective customers, doing risk and profitability analyses, supporting negotiations, etc. The business development manager's role described below is that of a mid-level manager who actively interfaces with prospective customers, presents them to internal management and engages in negotiations. Typically, either a director or vice president of business development closes final deals, although more discretion is given to managers at larger companies. Note that, of all functions, business development people are required to interface with more functions than other professionals. Their work encompasses understanding virtually all functions: the science behind a product/service offering well enough to communicate confidently, the markets to identify opportunities and measure risks, the valuation of a licensing agreement, and the regulatory and other constraints. And although communication skills are important in all functions, they are even more essential for business development professionals.

Name of position	Business Development Manager
Function	Business Development
Education level	BS in Microbiology, MBA
Company type and size	300 employees; mid-size company; < $150-$200 million in revenue
Hours per week	50-60
Salary range	$100K – $125K
Perks	Company car, performance bonus, reduced price stock offering

What are your responsibilities?

I am responsible for locating customers who fit our offering: manufacturing of small and large molecule technology for biotech companies. I coordinate clients to make sure there's a fit with respect to the financial, regulatory, liability, and scope of service parameters. Working out the terms for these parameters often leads to 40-50 page documents. Closing a deal involves two main phases: identifying the company, then negotiating the actual contract.

We break down the industry into several customer segments: virtual and small biotech companies, medium-size companies, and large biopharma companies. Each has different set of needs.

The virtual and small segment is the most promising since they typically don't have any process development or manufacturing infrastructure, insight into GMP or knowledge of FDA regulatory approval requirements.

Specifically, we take a gene, insert it into a cell strain, and express the protein to allow for testing in animals. Then, we manufacture it according to GMP guidelines. So basically, we fulfill the manufacturing step at the stage when a drug candidate is ready to move from the bench to clinical trials. We get involved mostly in Phase I and II, with some participation in Phase III. Although not a huge revenue generator currently, our strategy is that we will be the commercial producer for makers of drug candidates that ultimately make it to FDA approval.

What are the criteria for success in this position?

You have to have perseverance, be goal driven, organized, and good at prioritizing tasks and managing time. You also need to be able to speak the biotech language and have project management skills. Negotiation skills are essential. To be a strong negotiator, you have to have the ability to anticipate the other party's needs and attempt to ensure that your company's needs are as aligned as possible with those of the other party's. You also need to be able to be strong enough to know when to draw a line and stick to it.

What advice do you have for job seekers?

The best advice for people wanting to work in business development is to demonstrate that ability via their strategy and execution of that strategy in the search for a job, since a job search is very similar. Responding to ads and postings are certainly valid leads to a job, but a job search that demonstrates business development ability has two essential components: First, you have to be able to determine who is the key person making the hiring decision and give that person enough information about you so that they become willing to meet with you. Second, you have the negotiation where you try to convince that person of the value they would receive by hiring you. The final decision is often about what drives that person and what is driving their current needs."

The type of person who is most effective in business development is often an "enterprising personality, since it is expected you will be proactive, analytical, and structured, but also be able to meet people and communicate – essentially an introverted personality that can act as an extrovert when necessary.

A Day in the Life: Business Development Manager

8:00 a.m.: I spend half an hour reviewing what I've planned for the day and another half hour checking and responding to e-mail. There is no routine to my days. My days are divided between proactive and reactive work. Although you have much more control on the proactive side, I'm often on the reactive side of things. This makes my days much less predictable. You have to be able to plan both sides to be productive.

Proactive work: My typical proactive tasks include:

- Getting back to any potential customers
- Scheduling meetings with prospects
- Sending draft proposals to potential clients to go through the details in preparation for negotiating contract terms
- Conducting project review board meetings to screen potential projects at a high level (e.g., senior executives, subject matter

experts or SMEs) to make a go/no go decision. This involves collecting information, drafting, or editing proposals

- Conducting commercial review meetings with existing clients to review current projects and determine whether we are meeting our agreed-upon terms (usually either monthly or biweekly meetings)
- Coordinating and scheduling conferences and trade shows
- Regularly and routinely contacting key industry players who we may not have business with (i.e., maintaining relationships)

Reactive Work: My reactive work typically involves:

- Responding to potential client inquiries (phone, e-mail, referral) to set up meetings, collect information, draft proposals, review them with clients, respond to their questions, and set up the terms of the contract
- Setting up negotiations with internal clients (e.g., senior executives) as well as external clients

It's important to react in a structured way, but the points of reaction are not that predictable. The challenge is always scheduling, since multiple people with multiple schedules can make coordination unpredictable.

Business Development Manager Uppers and Downers

Uppers

Travel can be either a pro or a con, depending on whether you are single or have a family.

I am often in conversations with leading researchers, who are on the cutting-edge of science, discussing how products are going to be commercialized – that's exciting.

Bringing products to market that are helping to save people's lives is also very satisfying.

I like having the flexibility and freedom that comes from having a job with limited structure and a measure of unpredictability.

Downers

I am quite often the giver of bad news and the receiver of client reactions to that news. For example, when their schedule changes, and they don't make promised deliveries, that impacts everything we do, and often delays our ability to manufacture the product.

You also have to have a thick enough skin to not react to their disappointment and anger.

Bionformatics Analyst

Generally speaking, bioinformatics can be divided into two broad categories: statistical and applied. Statistical bioinformatics investigates new algorithms or ways of analyzing large volumes of data, and as such is more theoretical in orientation. Applied bioinformatics, on the other hand, uses such algorithms or programs to interpret real biological data generated by discovery research scientists. Two common types of data are microarray and sequencing data. An example of an applied bioinformatics project might be to determine the DNA sequence of a gene, or figuring out what letters go in what order.

One application of statistical bioinformatics is to write computer models to see how proteins fold, as they are produced or "expressed" from DNA. A computation-intensive activity, the model generates the math necessary to represent the protein graphically. From there, you can figure out what the protein's three-dimensional structure looks like. Another application might involve the mathematical modeling of evolution within a species. Here a variant of the Monte Carlo algorithm is used. In the chain method Monte Carlo, a self-propagating program, the data generated is fed back into the program. The whole procedure requires multiple computers and one calculation usually takes a month to complete.

We explain all this to put the work of the bioinformatics analyst we profile in perspective. Although most of his work is applied, the analyst notes that part of the center's mandate is also to develop new theoretical models. Note also that the academic center where this worker is located is funded by a private corporation, an example of the new forms of partnership evolving in the biotech world today.

Visit Vault at **www.vault.com** for insider company profiles, expert advice, career message boards, expert resume reviews, the Vault Job Board and more.

VAULT CAREER LIBRARY   **93**

Name of position	IT/Bioinformatics Analyst
Function	Bioinformatics
Education level	BA in Biology with a focus in Computational Biology
Company type and size	Part of a center in a university; funded by a corporation; group has 7 employees and 3 new analyst positions open
Hours per week	40-50 hours
Salary range	$40,000 – $50,000 (academic salary range)
Perks	Standard benefits package that comes with academic position; flexible work arrangement, where group members can work from home 2 days per week. This is standard for all group members.

What are your responsibilities?

I've been on the job for about a year. Our center runs a large-scale, high-throughput genome sequencing effort. When I first started the job, I was expected to learn how to access data in the different databases, figure out how data security worked, and run the same type of analysis with different data. For the first six months, I received a weekly list of things to do from my manager – for example, do a BLASTX analysis – on a particular data set. Our group typically meets at least twice a week to see how the analyses are going.

Gradually, I started out doing different analyses on the same data set. I've been on the job for a year now, and can apply 20 different analysis methods to analyze data sets. I've also been granted some leverage in what method to apply.

What are the criteria for success in this position?

First, you have to be interested in genetics. Second, you have to like being in front of a computer and not to want to do lab work. If you want to do lab work, you won't get hired, since the essence of the job is that you have to be in front of a computer.

You also have to be meticulous, independent, be willing to work on your own and at your own pace, and not mind doing the same task over and over. This is because you have to do the same analysis on different data. The ability to multitask is also important since you often have several different analyses going in any one week. Finally, you have to be able to write computer programs to help deal with repetitive tasks.

What advice do you have for job seekers?

If you are an undergraduate, determine what you like more – computer programming or biology. You have to like working on a computer. Find a school that either has a program or is very strong in both areas. Learn C and Perl. Perl is the language of bioinformatics. Take courses where you use various methods of analysis since you have to have some experience to get in the door.

If you are a graduate student, look for a specific program. If your institution does not have one and you want to stay there, you can customize your own program by merging computer science and biology. Be sure to also find a faculty mentor.

A Day in the Life: Bioinformatics Analyst

9:00 a.m.: Morning session: I usually spend the morning setting up and doing one analysis. This involves organizing data and reviewing lists of analyses to determine what to do next. Some analyzes can take from either a few hours to several days to complete. This is why I have to take special care to configure each set up right because mistakes can delay projects.

12:00 p.m.: Have lunch with the group to discuss results and share tips on running analyses.

1:00 p.m.: Afternoon session: Set up and run a second analysis. I usually have several analyses running simultaneously over a week's time.

5:00 p.m.: Meet with manager. Attend bi-weekly group meeting. Go over the status of ongoing analyses, report on progress in data analysis and interpretation, get direction on problems or issues that come up, get a heads-up on the next week's work.

6:00 p.m.: Commute home.

Visit Vault at **www.vault.com** for insider company profiles, expert advice, career message boards, expert resume reviews, the Vault Job Board and more.

VAULT CAREER LIBRARY   **95**

Bioinformatics Professional Uppers and Downers

Uppers

There's great flexibility in an academic environment. So the quality of work life is great. Also, you get to work on pretty cool computational hardware.

I can move on to new things after a project moves from us to the software developers.

Our manager is constantly exploring new ways of analyzing data, so, although the work is the same at first, you're also exposed to innovation.

Downers

Depending on where you work, if you are supporting a lot of researchers, they bring an idea to the group and the group works on it. That's okay but you can easily get overwhelmed with the number of projects, especially if the priorities keep changing.

Our Survey Says:
Lifestyle and Corporate Culture

CHAPTER 8

Corporate Culture

Although each company can claim to have its unique culture, most cultures are primarily a function of the size of the company: start-ups are high energy and intensely entrepreneurial; mid-size companies are often the "young adults" where order and systems begin to emerge; large companies often consciously organize business units into small, self-contained profit centers so as to recapture the entrepreneurial spark of the smaller firms.

Think often and intensely about how you work best and what kind of corporate culture will give you the best fit. Deciding what type of culture you will be happiest working in takes into account several important factors, including the extent of collaboration vs. competition, degree of team-oriented vs. independent work, the degree to which the organizational structure is relatively flat vs. more hierarchical, how much access to information employees are granted, how much people know about each other, and how "warm" or "cold" the environment feels.

Ultimately, Socrates' famous dictum, "know thyself!" applies. This self-assessment is an ongoing process that you will likely revisit at each stage of your career. What kind of temperament do you have? Do you like change? What is your tolerance for ambiguity? Do you need the certainty of an established career path, or would you prefer a more fluid environment where you can set your own direction?

These questions are especially important if you are thinking of entering the biotech industry, since many small research-oriented firms are likely to be taken over by larger firms if their technology is not fruitful or if venture cash runs dry. This means churning at the top, which can be disconcerting to those wanting a measure of predictability when they come to work every day.

Start-ups

An operations manager gives a few important insights on startups: "There's a huge mount of energy focused on acquiring funds and assembling the team. When funds do arrive, you set up the facility and do the work. There's no time to do an exhaustive talent search, so you have to hire people you know."

Visit Vault at www.vault.com for insider company profiles, expert advice, career message boards, expert resume reviews, the Vault Job Board and more.

VAULT CAREER LIBRARY

97

Day-to-day can be hectic, and there's a "premium for being able to multi-task. You also have to cover for people's shortcomings, since some may not have full skill sets." Typically, however, those who are hired in start-ups are "usually very smart and innovative problem solvers." Because of the inherent economic risks involved, "some venture capitalist (VCs) station an employee in a start up to keep an eye on the financials."

Small companies

As a firm transitions from a startup to a small company (say, 10-60 people), rapid growth often occurs on the scientific end – either from academic labs or other companies. In a small company, multi-tasking continues, since the support infrastructure is not fully in place. For example, the operations manager notes, "A scientist may be hired to clone genes, but have to take care of chemical waste or supervise a glasswasher or do ordering for the lab." Increasingly, however, the need for support for professionals is recognized and a lab manager and/or facility manager is hired at that point. The HR, purchasing, accounting, etc. functions are also gradually filled.

The operations manager notes, "Many founders like to invent things on their own, which leads to quirky management charts or unusual or atypical management structures. There is usually great loyalty to the original founders. A place for them will always be reserved, but sometimes that results in additional management issues as firm grows. As professional managers come in, however, things become more streamlined. A graceful founder will step aside at that point."

At startups and small companies, the facility itself may not be an optimal space to work in and working conditions might not be as comfortable or attractive as in more established companies. Crowded, shared offices – sometimes even shared desks – are not uncommon. There is less likely to be much attention to when work gets done and more flexibility with regard to the hours worked, since the expectation is that you will do weekend work when necessary.

"Experiments are timed to get results when the latter are needed – not to people's convenience," the operations manager continues. "There's a great camaraderie among the scientists and staff and real friendships form that last a long time. If you don't want to be friends with your co-workers, a startup may not be the best place for you to work." Another important aspect of a startup or very small company is that the contributions of each person are usually recognized, whereas in larger organizations, it is not always clear who is doing the work."

A vice president of business development echoes this attitude, "The corporate culture is positive and collegial. We [business development people] are the business facilitators of the scientists and others working with them, who are all trying to do the right science and make the right decisions."

Mid-sized to large companies

Mid-size firms have 60-300 employees, and are characterized by more organization, greater specialization of functions, and more distinct organizational units. See from the organization charts that business development functions become separated out from finance and administration and that the latter have more distinct groups. Reporting and accountability become more established; career paths and job descriptions are formalized. Other HR groups – benefits administration, recruiting, training, etc. – become more fleshed out. "Planning occurs around specific goals and milestones and the need to manage scientific research is more apparent, as is the need to train senior scientists in management. A poor or ineffective management can be very evident at this stage." Finally, boundaries are placed around flexible work schedules. One manager notes, "flextime is fine, but everyone has to be here between 10 a.m. and 3 p.m.."

As a company grows from 60 to 300, the type of people it attracts becomes different. "Creative geniuses can find that evolution restrictive," a senior manager asserts. "The academic mindset is very individualistic. In companies, you have to work on a team to achieve the company goal. There is always some pain associated with the transition to a more collaborative mode. When people were assigned narrow pieces of a project, as opposed to being involved in all stages, it's hard to maintain the sense of ownership. It takes a different type of scientist, one who can sustain a certain amount of repetitiveness and get a sense of satisfaction from seeing his/her work as part of a whole."

A mid-sized – or large – company environment can "be a much more logical place for the average worker looking for a relatively stable work environment." The trade-offs, however, can make a more significant impact on scientists accustomed to the professional visibility that is a norm in the academic world. As companies get larger, "the lab director presents papers, with only an acknowledgment to the people who actually did the work, so the visibility of bench scientists becomes more limited," a manager points out.

Visit Vault at **www.vault.com** for insider company profiles, expert advice, career message boards, expert resume reviews, the Vault Job Board and more.

VAULT CAREER LIBRARY   99

Since the downturn several years ago, biotech business models have been undergoing a gradual transformation. "In the early days of the industry, most people didn't 'get' that companies were economic entities. That has really changed in recent years," says one business development manager. Specifically, this means that companies are moving away from strategies that use venture capital funding for protracted periods of time (usually 10-15 years) before commercializing a product to one that stresses bringing in a revenue stream from products or services as discovery research is underway. Consequently, the attitudes toward research itself have needed to evolve, as scientists are increasingly encouraged to find ways of leveraging their technology platform to help the company survive as an economic entity. A business development executive comments, "The industry is definitely maturing."

Compensation and Lifestyle

Basic compensation

Most companies offer a full complement of benefits, including several weeks of vacation, sick leave, compensation time, education reimbursement, employee training and development and 401(k) retirement plans. Some companies provide stock options (depending on the job classification) and most companies encourage continuing education.

Since the biotech industry depends on highly skilled workers, employers are willing to consider various incentives to attract and retain workers. Among these incentives are recruiting bonuses, overtime incentives, and access to ongoing training and professional development.

Whatever employment level, it is useful to know how the position you are entering is compensated relative to similar positions at other companies. A useful resource to compare salaries, bonuses, and benefits can be found at this web site: http://www.salary.com. Doing a salary comparison analysis greatly empowers the employee and gives you the information you need to negotiate the best terms for a position you are entering. Salary information also helps you know how your salary is progressing relative to others in similar positions around the U.S.

Perks

Most companies offer performance bonuses for executives and senior managers. Although many companies still offer stock options, the price of many biotech equities remain relatively low compared to the 1990s. In addition, as one top recruiter points out, many managers and executives have become willing to forego "equity stakes for cash."

If a prospective employer offers you stock options as a form of compensation, look long and hard at whether your job can affect the stock price. If you are interviewing for a research associate job, your responsibilities are very far removed from having any effect – either positive or negative. If, however, you are interviewing for a CFO position (in which case, we won't ask why you need to read this section), your decisions much more directly impact Wall Street's assessment of the company. Management of cash-strapped companies often feel it can lure workers into working long hours without extra compensation if they offer stock options as a way to motivate employees. If the company falters, the options will be worthless and they get your labor anyway. If the company thrives, you get a small piece of the action. Either way, the worker incurs the risk and uncertainty. Our conclusion: caveat emptor.

More traditional perks include company cars and subsidized cafeterias. Business development and people in sales-oriented functions sometimes have use of company cars to ease the cost of contacting potential partners and co-marketers. Many companies have subsidized cafeterias that serve breakfast and lunch at reduced prices. Increasingly, companies also understand the benefits of employee fitness, and either have fitness facilities or offer subsidized subscriptions to gyms. Considering the extended hours many companies expect of their employees, these facilities can help maintain morale and reduce the general stress level.

Travel

The extent of travel in biotech depends on the business function. Business development people need to travel probably more often than people in other functions to seek out and meet partners, negotiate alliances, develop relationships with co-marketers, etc. A vice president of business development notes, "Travel can be difficult for some people and there is 50 percent travel for most jobs in the field." Sales jobs are essentially field-based and require extensive travel. Depending on the role, marketing people are sometimes called upon to travel occasionally.

Visit Vault at www.vault.com for insider company profiles, expert advice, career message boards, expert resume reviews, the Vault Job Board and more.

VAULT CAREER LIBRARY   101

Dress code

Most biotech companies, especially the smaller, discovery research oriented ones, are fairly casual in dress style. As the smaller biotechs come into contact with Big Pharma either as partners or as wholly owned business units, the tilt toward conservatism becomes more evident. Dress code also varies by function. R&D staff, with a focus on laboratory work, can dress fairly casually from day to day. Functions requiring either client contact or contact with investors and media professionals – business development, sales, marketing, corporate communications, etc. – require a more polished appearance.

Socializing and networking

With ongoing industry consolidation, qualified talent at a premium and the industry gradually moving toward an alliance model of specialty companies – not unlike the computer industry – the level and scope of networking events in biotech is extensive. Monthly social events (e.g., BiotechTuesdays in Boston) bring industry people together in casual settings. Web sites (see Appendix X: Resources) and online newsletters (e.g., BioWorld Online and FierceBiotech) help disseminate industry developments. Networking vehicles and social events provide the platform from which people make contacts with prospective employers and potential alliances are explored. Finally, the sheer youthfulness of workers and the often-heavy demands placed on people working in entrepreneurial settings creates an ongoing demand for fun.

Employment contracts

Traditionally, employment contracts were made between companies and senior executives. With turbulence in the economy and job security a virtual oxymoron in many industries, employment contracts are being drafted further down the organization into the middle manager ranks. Whereas it is a good idea to put down in writing any special terms under which you accept a job, most large companies don't draft employment agreements with professional and technical staff. Instead, they opt to explain the full complement of expectations required of an employee and benefits received as a result of meeting those expectations. In smaller companies or start-ups, or if you have any reservations about a hiring company's management, it is probably a good precaution to lay out the terms of your employment.

All United States-based companies have to comply with U.S. Labor Relations laws (i.e., affirmative action, non-discrimination, worker's compensation, etc.). Many company web sites have features that ask people to identify themselves by gender and race after submitting resumes online. These completely optional features help companies understand their applicant pool better and comply with labor laws. Remember, though, that during an interview, the interviewer cannot ask you about personal and lifestyle issues without breaking Federal labor laws. We're referring to religion, sexual orientation, national origin, ethnic identity, etc. So, it goes without saying, but we're going to say it anyway, don't volunteer information that can put your candidacy in jeopardy. If you are asked a question that makes you even a little uncomfortable, throw it back by asking (in an even tone and with a positive attitude) the interviewer to explain the relevance of the question to the position. That will alert the person on the other side of the desk that you know what's going on. Generally, however, interviewers are well trained on these issues and will not consciously ask anything that will put their companies at risk.

Compensation for executives

We're including this section so that you can get some perspective on the scope of compensation and incentives given to people at the top. We're also taking the numbers from a public site, as opposed to an industry group. The figures are based on annual median total compensation and stock option values given to biotech and pharmaceutical executives.

Position	Salary	Bonus	Long-term incentive payment	Stock-option value
Chief executive officer	$300K	$132K	$965K	$1,374K
Chairman of the board	230K	89K	N/A	235K
Chief operating officer	250K	83K	1,625K	888K
General manager	267K	223K	416K	1,028K
Chief financial officer	185K	48K	1,056K	400K
General counsel	230K	75K	219K	784K
Research and development executive	206K	45K	311K	717K

Visit Vault at **www.vault.com** for insider company profiles, expert advice, career message boards, expert resume reviews, the Vault Job Board and more.

VAULT CAREER LIBRARY   **103**

Position	Salary	Bonus	Long-term incentive payment	Stock-option value
Biopharmaceutical-product-development executive	180K	40K	N/A	454K
Clinical/medical-affairs executive	212K	50K	30K	444K
Regulatory affairs/quality-assurance executive	175K	30K	N/A	264K
Operations executive	166K	38K	382K	422K
Sales and marketing executive	179K	54K	N/A	292K
Marketing/business-development executive	180K	39K	377K	525K
Miscellaneous executive functions*	170K	49K	1,109K	280K

Note: Figures rounded off to nearest $1,000.
Source: http://www.careerjournal.com/salaryhiring

Sources: A Survey of the Use of Biotechnology in U.S. Industry, Technology Administration Office of Public Affairs, U.S. Department of Commerce, 2003 (http://www.technology.gov), Standard & Poor's industry surveys and company reports

GETTING HIRED

Use the Internet's
MOST TARGETED
job search tools.

Vault Job Board

Target your search by industry, function, and experience level, and find the job openings that you want.

VaultMatch Resume Database

Vault takes match-making to the next level: post your resume and customize your search by industry, function, experience and more. We'll match job listings with your interests and criteria and e-mail them directly to your inbox.

VAULT
> the most trusted name in career information™

The Hiring Process

CHAPTER 9

Biotech Hiring Basics

A wide range of opportunities

Because biotechnology applications exist across healthcare, agriculture, food processing, and industry, virtually any college major in a scientific and life science is likely to find a biotech application. Biotech companies per se are most likely to have healthcare applications, and as we've already noted, are essentially mid-cap pharmaceutical companies. Typical college majors among biotech professionals include chemistry, biology, physics, biochemistry, bioengineering, among many others. You can also get an undergraduate degree in bioinformatics. Potential employers span across government, private industry, and academia. That pretty much covers most of the employment universe, so you may well feel bewildered about how to proceed.

Interconnected institutions

A lucky few understand themselves early enough to have clarity on these issues while still in their teens. If you are one of those and feeling a bit smug, rest assured that, although you have an edge on your colleagues, the work world you are heading into is more complex than it was just a few years ago. Universities are increasingly looking to leverage the intellectual capital of their researchers to land licensing deals with the private sector. Since much research is funded by the Federal government (in other words, your taxpayer dollars), the Feds have an incentive to see some of that money get recycled in the private sector economy, through goods and services that can improve the lives and standards of living of ordinary Americans.

Thus, most universities have technology licensing offices that help its scientists set up licensing and entrepreneurial deals with the private sector. The idea is to commercialize the science into products, devices, processes, and products that are useful to consumers. What this translates into is increased revenues for private sector companies, which in turn increases the tax base for the Federal government. From the private sector's perspective, venture capitalists are looking increasingly to late-stage research that's just about ready to be commercialized. That shortens their period of investment, which means they can cash out faster and invest limited partner dollars into the next promising project. Academic researchers whose work fits those criteria are attractive candidates. This is because someone else (the Feds) picked up the tab for that uncertain early-stage phase when there is great uncertainty as to whether anything practical will come out of a research idea. Funding from private equity can now go right into creating the practical from the theoretical.

The upshot is that, whatever sector you choose to work in – government, private industry, or academia – you are likely to forge links with people in other sectors.

A passion for biotech

How do you get hired? The most important thing to remember is to know what really excites you, since, as biotech recruiters point out, the most successful candidates exhibit "passion about the work," and are willing "to work hard and do what it takes to succeed, since many companies are lightly staffed." To get hired, you also need to express an abiding "desire to make a difference in the health and well being of others." But the more challenging part of getting hired in biotech is that educational requirements and work experience are among the most specific of any industry. That's because the science on which biotech companies are based is still relatively new and the number of graduates from biotech-related programs in higher educational institutions relatively few. That actually works to the advantage of younger people, who can tailor an academic program to what the industry needs.

It's worth repeating that "biotechnology" is a set of technologies that are applied throughout several industries. So when making a career choice, review the main areas of application discussed in The Scoop: healthcare, agriculture, food processing, and industrial processing. If you are still in college, know you like the life sciences, and are contemplating a future in either discovering or promoting new treatments for hitherto genetically based diseases, then you'll want to consider carefully the kind of education and other credentialing we discuss here.

A word about scientific leadership

As financing pressures shorten the timelines needed to bring a product to market, a new profile of scientist and scientific leader is emerging, according to top industry recruiters. In the business of developing drugs three factors must come together – management, science, and people. "Scientists in today's environment need to do more than good science," says a top scientific recruiter. "They need to have more accountability – i.e., to enable the team to meet milestones or identifiable timelines that in turn generate revenues and additional capital. We need the brilliant minds who also understand that the company has to earn revenues."

Broadly speaking, "we are seeing a shift in the philosophy of scientific management from one focused purely on science to one that compensates people for meeting business goals in addition to creating great science. "The leaders that will emerge will have both sets of attributes – the ability to lead teams to meet management goals and to create great scientific results. The key for scientific leaders is to know when the let go and cut out unpromising avenues of research. This shift will create efficiencies, as more capital becomes available to explore more promising leads. It's all about understanding the scientific bench work in a business context."

What this means is that, for those aspiring to a career as scientific leaders, it is essential to broaden your perspective earlier than later, so that you will be more effective in the positions of responsibility you will eventually land.

Geography matters

One last general note about getting hired – if you are intent on working in biotech, you might want to keep in mind the geographic concentration of the industry. In 2002, six states – California, Massachusetts, Maryland, North Carolina, Pennsylvania and New Jersey – employed about 68 percent of biotech workers, according to a Department of Commerce study. This concentration of employers is due to the availability of venture capital, local entrepreneurship, a tendency of researchers to want to work in close proximity to each other, and the availability of academic programs, which produce pools of highly skilled labor.

Other factors also contribute to this concentration and might influence your decision as to where to target your job search. In nearly all cases, states with concentrations of employers got there both as a result of favorable business conditions established by state governments and a dedicated effort to attract a share of the present and future biotech employment pool. The reasoning is that, with highly skilled jobs will come new taxpayers that will earn higher salaries, and thus, broaden the state's tax base. In addition to government's contribution, employer-rich states have also made an equally dedicated effort to develop academic programs that will serve the industry. With a readily available pool of qualified candidates, employers can draw on local people for most entry to mid-level spots.

Hiring Process for Students and Recent Grads

If you are a student, run, don't walk, to your career center. There, you will find postings on when recruiters will be on campus, what internships and co-op working programs are available, and what full-time positions will open up when you graduate. Once you have this basic information, it is up to you to follow-up on the opportunities available. How helpful the people in these centers are in actually working with you to find a job is likely to be uneven from one institution to another. It is also likely that their knowledge of specific industries will be limited. In all cases, understanding how to best use this resource will save you time and energy.

Individual departments are likely to know much more about specific opportunities, especially if the college or university has a strong program in the life sciences. Your best bet is to look out for information about internships, part-time jobs and other opportunities within the department office and speak with life sciences professors. They will likely be much more familiar with requests that come through their departmental office than career services staff and will be able to guide you.

Most companies post positions on the "Careers" page of their web sites. In addition to listings, many companies have additional useful information, such as interview tips and guidance on resumes. The internships section of this guide contains URLs for a number of company sites. Browse through these sites to get a better sense of what a target company is looking for in entry-level applicants. Note that it's always a good idea to follow the directions on company web sites – if the company says to apply online only, then comply and don't send a paper resume. It might not get entered into their database and you will have not made the best first impression.

Co-op programs

Large companies often sponsor co-op programs with academic institutions; these programs are designed to give students a taste of what a field is like while they are still completing undergraduate studies. Co-op programs provide a salary, and hence help students subsidize their education and get a head start in adding practical experience to their resumes while still in school. The duration of these programs is the standard academic year – September to June – and thus, co-op programs require a greater commitment on both the student and employer than the relatively shorter period of the standard internship (10 weeks).

If you are interested in a co-op program, remember that it will likely be with a large company. Small, discovery research-oriented biotech firms usually don't have the resources to support co-op students since many of them operate on venture capital funding and have not yet marketed a product. Big pharma companies have both internships and co-op programs. Your best bet is to apply to a large pharma company that has also acquired a biotech unit (e.g., Johnson and Johnson's Centocor) and see about landing an assignment in that unit. Alternatively, the larger biotechs (e.g., Genentech, Biogen) are increasingly taking on the characteristics of Big Pharma companies with each passing year. If a company you are interested in does not have a co-op program, float the idea with an advisor or professor in your academic department to see if your institution is willing to work with the company to set one up. Proactivity is often rewarded.

While it is not mandatory to have work experience before graduation to get a job in the biotech industry, having early industry exposure will both facilitate and shorten your search. Biotech jobs have very specific skill sets, which means that the more focused candidates will have an edge in getting hired. Remember, too, that industry skills are homegrown, since the barriers to entry are higher than in most industries. This makes prospective workers with direct experience more credible than workers crossing over from other industries.

Internships for Students

Internships are another great way to get your foot in the door. An assistant scientist got her position this way: "I had an internship the summer before senior year, then was offered a position during senior year. Alumni contacts and job fairs are also useful. My department at college allowed us to have an industrial experience in lieu of writing a senior thesis. The department had contacts in HR departments in industry. One of my professors was an advisor to the company that hired me, and he forwarded my resume to the HR department."

Many major biotech companies, as well as big pharmaceutical companies have internships to help develop talent right from the start of your career. Internships usually involve doing work in functional areas that is similar to that which is normally done in full-time jobs and offer a great opportunity to gain exposure at a major company. In addition to helping you develop your skills in a specific functional area, an internship will permit you to work in the collaborative, team-oriented environment that is the norm in the business world today.

Getting an internship is probably the single most effective tactic in meeting your long-term strategy of landing a job in the biotech industry. Although finding one can seem overwhelming at first, identifying the right resources and getting started early will help you meet your goal. Academic departments, professors and career services are the most immediate sources of suitable internships. If you are entering your junior year of college, getting to know the seniors who have just completed an internship will be well worth your time, as they will be able to evaluate their experience and give you tips on the sponsoring company.

Also be sure to contact the state biotech organizations for further direction. Their mandate is to support and promote the industry within the state and hence will have the inside track on what is going on in your region. State biotech organizations – especially those whose states are major employers – usually host annual networking events. The purpose is to bring people together and present the latest advances and most provocative issues in the industry. The state offices can provide you with a calendar of events.

The appendix at the back of this book lists numerous other sites – both academic and professional – in the U.S. and other countries. We have included them to give even more access to insiders. They are especially useful if you do not live in an area of employer concentration since they provide a contact point for local news and information about biotech-related activities.

Grooming yourself for an internship is not unlike doing the same for a job interview. The most promising candidates will show signs of interest in the industry as well as solid academic achievement and good self-management skills. Distinguishing yourself from other potential candidates is a matter of leveraging what you do best. Do you like to write? Produce a well-researched article for an online publication. Are you comfortable meeting new people? Volunteer to help organize events at professional associations. Think of yourself as the ultimate nerd? Seek out tutoring jobs either at the college or secondary school level. Lots of parents are desperate to have their children learn math and science. These suggestions are specific ways you can demonstrate what you do best; they will be highlighted in the recommendations written on your behalf and will impress hiring managers.

Specific Company Internships

The listing below is but a small subset of the many companies that offer internships for students. We have summarized the main points, but for a full understanding, go to the links identified.

Abbott Laboratories

Abbott has a large and well-regarded internship program. Over 250 students each year across the United States have the chance to win an Abbott internship in most fields of science, finance/accounting, information technology, engineering, and sales. The best time to connect with Abbott is when a representative comes to campus to visit. Check with your career services office to find the exact date. Electronic resumes are accepted at:

http://jobs.brassring.com/EN/ASP/TG/cim_home.asp

Resumes for summer internships are accepted between September 1 and February 28.

Amgen

Amgen has two types of summer internships: one for finance and the other for marketing. Targeted for students between the first and second year of business school, these internships also require two or more years of relevant work experience in a corporate environment. Experience in either biotechnology, pharmaceuticals or healthcare is preferred but not required. Resumes are accepted in January and February. Apply at:

http://wwwext.amgen.com/career/resumeFinanceIntern.html

Biogen

Biogen offers a summer internship program in all life science disciplines as well as in finance and marketing. Biogen accepts students at various stages of higher education, but requires either basic or advanced science courses for laboratory positions. Resumes are accepted only via e-mail at: biogeninterns@trm.brassring.com

Include a cover letter expressing your field of interest, a list of science courses completed with the grades you've earned, and a brief statement as to why you wish to work for Biogen. Resumes for summer internships are accepted up to April 15.

Eli Lilly

Eli Lilly has internship positions for chemistry, biology, pharmacy, engineering/manufacturing operations, occupational health and safety, finance, marketing, human resources, and information technology/computer science. Resumes are accepted at:

http://campuszone.lilly.com/intern_program.html

Like other big companies, the best way to connect with Eli Lilly is through an on-campus visit from a company recruiter. Eli Lilly prefers to recruit actively on campuses, so check with your career services office to see when a representative will be on site.

Genentech

Genentech has a broad internship program covering virtually all life science and business disciplines. Internships are provided for the summer after sophomore year for students planning to return to full-time study the following year and who are majoring in the life or chemical sciences or life or science engineering. In addition to working on a project team focused on either research, development, or manufacturing, interns formally present their work at the end of the summer. In addition to summer interns, many departments also host yearlong interns. Resumes for summer internships are accepted up to April 30 before the program begins.

Apply at: http://www.genentech.com/gene/careers/college/internships

Genzyme

Genzyme offers a summer internship program in the life sciences and core business functions of finance, marketing, and information technology. It has programs for both undergraduates and MBA and graduate students. Genzyme also has a mandatory orientation program prior to the start of the internship. Apply at:

http://www.genzyme.com/corp/careers/fulltime_positions.asp

Gilead Sciences

Gilead Sciences offers internships in medicinal chemistry, biology, metabolism, and protein chemistry at its Foster City, Calif., site for college and university students who are entering their junior year with a B average or better and have completed at least one lab course. Resumes are accepted via e-mail:

careers@gilead.com.

GlaxoSmithKline

GlaxoSmithKline offers a summer intern program for college, graduate, and MBA students. The program for MBA students offers positions in brand management, business development, and marketing analytics and is meant to be an extension of the Management Development Program (MDP) for full-time recruitment. The program for college and graduate students offers positions at the Raleigh, N.C., area and Greater Philadelphia, Pa., sites. All applicants must apply via the web site only; hard copy resumes will not be accepted.

Resumes are accepted at:
http://www.gsk.com/join/us-university/university_us_summermba.htm
http://www.gsk.com/join/us-university/university_us_undergrad.htm

Johnson & Johnson

Johnson & Johnson has both full- and part-time internship positions within its various companies, which it offers to qualified students three times a year – during the spring, summer, and fall semesters. Resumes are accepted at:

http://www.jnj.com/careers/interns.html

Pfizer

Pfizer has an extensive internship program consisting of both standard summer positions as well as six-month-long assignments, where students receive academic credit in addition to real-world experience. Internships are available in most major functional areas, including research and development, marketing, finance, human resources, production, sales, and legal. Since each division processes its own internships, contact the main web site for specific information. You can also send resumes to:

Human Resources

Pfizer Inc

Pfizer Global Pharmaceuticals

Attn: [type of internship]

235 E. 42nd St. – 13th Floor

New York, NY 10017-5755

In addition, resumes for summer internships are accepted at:
http://www.pfizerrdgrad.com/

Roche Laboratories

Roche offers summer internships from June 15 to August 15 for undergraduate juniors and seniors for biochemistry, cell biology, analytical chemistry, medicinal chemistry, molecular biology, pharmacology, and bioinformatics. Resumes for summer internships are accepted between November and February. Interviews are held between March and April. Resumes are accepted at:

paloalto.interns@roche.com

Wyeth Pharmaceuticals

Wyeth offers summer internships and actively recruits on campus for both college students and MBA candidates. Contact the career services office to find out when recruiters will be on campus. Send your resume and cover letter to:

Wyeth@Trackcareers.com

Or fax these documents to (419) 429-6074. Be sure to include your area of interest.

Internships at Other Institutions

In addition to specific companies, you might want to check out internships in the large federally funded medical research institutions. The National Institutes of Health has numerous internships in biotechnology, medical research, and various other disciplines. The NIH provides these useful links:

- http://www.training.nih.gov/student/sip/asp/sipquestions.asp: dedicated to answering questions about student summer internships

- NIH Biotechnology Research Training Program: http://www.nihbiotech.rice.edu/intern.cfm

You might also try the following resources to help you identify an internship that's right for you.

New York Center for Biotechnology

Internships in biomedical engineering and biotechnology companies in New York State

http://www.lifc.bio.sunysb.cdu/biotcch/ps/intcrn.html

MBC Careers & Internships Directory

http://www.massbio.org/careers

Internships-USA

http://www.internships-usa.com

CollegeGrad.com – Internship Postings

Information on internships, co-ops, summer jobs, and part-time work in the U.S. and internationally

http://www.collegegrad.com/internships/

InternJobs.com National Student Internships and Careers

National database of internships for students and recent graduates

http://www.internjobs.com

Visit Vault at **www.vault.com** for insider company profiles, expert advice, career message boards, expert resume reviews, the Vault Job Board and more.

VAULT CAREER LIBRARY   **117**

Hiring Process for Experienced Professionals

There is no single hiring process for experienced professionals. However, since many biotech jobs have very specific job requirements, many companies go through headhunters to identify qualified candidates. Refer to the appendix for a listing of biotech recruiters. Because the industry is consolidating, you will find many search firms that cover both pharmaceuticals and biotechnology jobs. In addition, some search firms concentrate on specific functional areas, such as sales/marketing, clinical research, or discovery research.

A manufacturing/operations manager reported that she "was contacted by a recruiter, who concentrated in biotech; they really understood what the position required. They also had a deep network of people – both potential candidates and people who knew potential candidates. I had three interviews:

- An initial screening interview
- An interview with peers and colleagues
- A final interview with the CEO

Then I was offered the position. The entire process was fairly quick, taking approximately one week." This process is not atypical of managerial jobs in the industry.

Many jobs for experienced professionals are not advertised since successful candidates are normally identified through private referrals. This places a great premium for the job hunter on networking within the industry. Going to professional meetings, reading professional journals, and going to networking events are two ways to keep up. Because biotech is a relatively young industry and has attracted workers in their 20s and 30s, networking social events are not uncommon, especially in larger cities such as Boston and San Francisco. Learn to interpret news bulletins for clues about prospective opportunities: For example, comments about a company's growth means that they will likely be staffing up and will be looking to hire people.

Alumni networks are another very effective way to unlock the "hidden" job market. Most academic institutions have alumni web sites, which in turn contain both "job search" and "alumni search" links. Some employers list jobs at alumni sites in schools whose graduates they routinely hire. This is a great resource and one you should make every effort to access. The "alumni search" link will help you network, since biographical and contact information is usually available. From there, you can find out who is working in what industry, send an introductory letter, and inquire about doing informational interviews before you actually need a job. Doing this as early as possible will give you insight and access to people later on. Different institutions have different rules on access to these sites; some limit access until after you graduate. Find out what access you have and when you will have it.

Changing Careers into Biotech

If the prospect of changing careers leaves you feeling so queasy that you want to jump into bed and draw the covers over your head, think again. Career experts predict that young people entering the workforce to day are likely to have as many six careers in their working lives.

The most significant rewards of career transitions are likely to be internal and non-monetary. A better fit with your primary colleagues and work environment, more personal satisfaction from the new focus relative to the old, greater self-confidence and self-esteem, and generally, an overall greater sense of happiness with life – these are the main rewards of successful career transitions.

On the other hand, career transitions can be costly both in monetary terms, as a result of the need for retooling, and in terms of professional status, as you will likely have to reenter the workplace at a less-senior level than you were in the old career.

"Most recruiters work with people inside their existing skill set," asserts a leading recruiter. "It's pretty tough to transition to new careers in this economy. Most companies don't want to hire someone who has to ramp up. There are too many people with the specific skills sets needed."

In a scientific field like biotechnology, the three main possible career transitions involve transitions from:

- Scientific to non-scientific field (e.g., discovery research scientist to operations manager)

- Technical to administrative field (e.g., research scientist to business development)

- A discipline/field outside the biological sciences to one within the industry

Below are some examples of how you might carry out a career transition.

Case 1: A scientist wishes to leave discovery research to focus on developing products for commercialization. This transition is one that involves moving from basic science to applied science and engineering. Although it may seem straightforward, this type of transition requires a fundamental shift in intellectual focus, which is often difficult for many people.

Strategy: Coursework in engineering is a definite plus, and may be required for senior positions. In addition to academic work, exposure to engineering environments is critical, as it will provide you with the crucial "reality checks" needed to make informed choices.

Assessment: At the heart of this transition is a need to solve more concrete problems than basic research allows and a desire to obtain solutions to practical problems. It also helps to be passionate about bringing a promising product or technology "to the real world."

Case 2: A Master's level chemist wants to focus more on business issues. This is a common transition, which many scientists at the BS/MS level make after a few years at the bench. For scientists who choose to not earn a Ph.D., career prospects are limited. Many opt to enter administrative fields instead.

Strategy: An excellent way into such a field – finance, sales, marketing, etc. – is to earn an MBA. For those with only a few years of experience at the bench, a regular, full-time program is probably the most attractive option, as it will give you an opportunity to immerse yourself in new concepts and network with colleagues who are also making their own transitions. For others with substantial experience, or for those who do not want to disrupt their earning power, an executive MBA (EMBA) program might be a better option. An EMBA program will expose you to other working professionals and give you a rich source of contacts for opportunities post-graduation. A final alternative is a custom EMBA program; these are designed for specific companies to train business executives more narrowly focused on the company's needs.

Assessment: Biotech companies often require MBA degrees for their most senior executive positions.

Case 3: An intellectual property attorney specializing in electronics and high-technology wants to transition into biopharmaceuticals.

Having a JD plus experience in prosecuting patents for high-tech firms is a significant achievement by itself. Our attorney, who had originally planned to go to medical school, already had several undergraduate-level pre-med courses. Biotech firms, however, are extremely particular about who handles their patent, licensing, and other intellectual property issues, as that often represents the core of their value. Most companies require a Ph.D. in a biological science followed by a JD – ideally, in that order, according to industry insiders. So how to make the transition?

Strategy: Our resourceful attorney identified the technology licensing offices at several universities with well-established biotechnology research programs. He applied simultaneously to a Ph.D. program and to a licensing officer position. The university permits employees to attend courses during the day and reimburses tuition expenses. In addition, the office encouraged his efforts and was generous in designing a work schedule that was flexible enough to attend classes during the day.

Assessment: This strategy will keep you earning a salary, while completing coursework. The schedule is full and most of your waking hours will be consumed with work and study. However, the end goal – a dual professional credential of PhD/JD – is a most valuable asset combination and will position you well to handle the intellectual assets of a biotech company of your choice.

Visit Vault at **www.vault.com** for insider company profiles, expert advice, career message boards, expert resume reviews, the Vault Job Board and more.

VAULT CAREER LIBRARY   **121**

Qualifications for Lab Research Careers

CHAPTER 10

Within each of the three main paths in laboratory research careers – discovery research, bioinformatics, and animal sciences – there exist different types of jobs that each require a specific set of education and experience. Some jobs have several tiers and, thus, allow you to be promoted as you gain experience. But on the job experience only goes so far in lab-oriented careers – at some point, you will need an advanced degree to move forward.

Whatever the specific title, research jobs are grouped into two classifications: those requiring a BS/MS and those requiring a Ph.D. Although it is not altogether impossible for a very experienced person at the BS/MS level to land a position that usually requires a Ph.D., that scenario is highly unlikely and not one that we recommend you consider. Understanding these barriers to entry based on educational achievement early is really important, as it will help you manage your expectations and plan for your future better. Another useful point is that lab-research positions are essentially the same throughout the industry, but specific titles can differ from company to company

Discovery research

The progression of discovery research positions typically follows the track of research associate, scientist, senior scientist, and principal scientist. (Some companies use different titles.) There are two points of entry if you have no previous experience. Typically, you will need a Master's degree to break into a research associate job and a Ph.D. to break into a scientist job.

However, it's possible to get a research associate job with only an undergraduate degree. Target the research associate job while still in college by seeking out summer internships and/or co-op programs to get deep biotech experience. This early exposure will also give you the chance to see whether you are comfortable in a business-oriented research environment and test your desire to work toward an advanced scientific degree (or perhaps spur you to transition out of research into any one of the many non-lab oriented careers.) In addition, such proactive moves on your part will give you the inside track on getting hired, since employers already know how their interns and co-op workers performed on the job, and hence, can direct them more readily to available openings after graduation.

Visit Vault at **www.vault.com** for insider company profiles, expert advice, career message boards, expert resume reviews, the Vault Job Board and more.

VAULT CAREER LIBRARY   123

The research associate job provides key laboratory research support to the senior scientific staff. Research associates make observations, gather and analyze data, and interpret results. They work under direct supervision of group, but often have some discretion in carrying out their assigned tasks. They also prepare technical reports, summaries, protocols, and quantitative analyses.

The scientist job is the senior researcher position in the R&D function. At this level, scientists are expected to possess in-depth knowledge of the theories and concepts in their areas of expertise. They are also expected to be able to apply these concepts to solve a broad range of complex problems of interest to the company that employs them. Scientists design, implement, and execute scientific research and development projects within a research team. They write research articles and participate in scientific conferences and symposia. Scientists also often provide the guidance and training needed by research associates.

Bioinformatics

Bioinformatics positions usually have titles like scientist/engineer, analyst/programmer, and molecular modeler. Most jobs require a BS/MS level of education, with a stronger preference for the Master's level. Typical majors include bioinformatics, statistics, biochemistry, mathematics, molecular biology, computer science, computational chemistry, and molecular or computational biology. In addition, fluency in computer languages, knowledge of relational and public databases and system administration will make you more competitive. In recent years, Ph.D. programs that specialize in bioinformatics have been cropping up, but people working in the field will tell you that you don't need one to do the work, especially for analyst or programmer jobs. In the academic world, that will put you out of kilter with peers in other disciplines. In the private sector, however, where these skills are very much in demand, you are likely to land a job shortly after the BS level if you graduate from a dedicated program. You do, however, need experience and all jobs need at least some degree of experience to break in.

You can break in with as little as one year of experience for the scientist/engineer and analyst/programmer jobs. As with entry-level research associate jobs, you can target bioinformatics jobs while still in college via internships and co-ops. Due to the nature of the work, it is also wise to seek out part-time or consulting work developing computational biology applications and to acquire proficiency in the computing languages most often used in the field (e.g., C/C++, Perl, SQL, HTML, or JAVA).

Because bioinformatics is inherently interdisciplinary, academic programs steep students in both biology and computing methods before integrating the two disciplines. The industry relies heavily on computing techniques, particularly with the advent of high-throughput screening techniques in the 1990s, where data is generated on thousands of compounds at once. Potential employers include traditional high-tech employers like IBM. Specific areas of employment include data mining/development, database administration, systems engineering, research technology, product management, applications development, and bioinformatics technology.

Bioinformatics careers require the ability to analyze complex data sets and managing databases, as well as software design and development. Only a handful of programs exist in the United States and are included below. According to a bioinformatics manager, "Bioinformatics programs cropping up in many university programs emphasize either statistical or applied bioinformatics. It's good to have a sense of what your program emphasizes, so that you can direct your studies better." Note that since this is a new field, some academic institutions (e.g., The Keck Centers) have created programs through joint efforts. In such cases, students will have a "home" department but a concentration in the new discipline.

If you are intent on pursuing a newly created program, seek out current students. Ask about how well the program is administered, how easy it is to have access to resources at collaborating institutions, how readily professors and administrators are willing to let you in on activities at other schools, and how much time and attention you can expect.

Graduate Bioinformatics Programs

Program	Features
Boston University (www.bu.edu/eng)	MS and Ph.D. in bioinformatics 30 faculty and several centers and departments Program has won National Science Foundation support
Bioinformatics and Computational Biology at George Mason University	Ph.D. in bioinformatics and computational biology

Visit Vault at www.vault.com for insider company profiles, expert advice, career message boards, expert resume reviews, the Vault Job Board and more.

VAULT CAREER LIBRARY   125

Program	Features
Bioinformatics at the University of Manchester School of Biological Sciences	MS in bioinformatics and computational molecular biology
Computational Molecular Biology Graduate Studies at Rutgers University	Ph.D. program Joint effort of Rutgers and the University of Medicine and Dentistry of New Jersey
Computational Molecular Biology Program at Washington University in St. Louis	Ph.D. program Computational molecular biology and genome analysis
W. M. Keck Center for Advanced Training in Computational Biology at Pittsburgh, Pa.	Graduate and postdoctoral programs in computational biology Collaboration among Carnegie Mellon, the Pittsburgh Supercomputing Center, and the University of Pittsburgh
The W.M. Keck Center for Computational Biology in Houston, Texas	Graduate and postdoctoral programs in computational biology Collaboration through three partner institutions: Baylor College of Medicine, Rice University, and the University of Houston

Although bioinformatics and discovery research are currently two separate groups in biotech companies, according to a bioinformatics manager, "The two functions are slowly merging, with students in the discovery research disciplines being exposed to bioinformatics methods as early as the undergraduate years. This is happening because computational methods of analysis are so crucial to interpreting the data generated by laboratory scientists." This means that developing sophistication in reading and interpreting the outputs of advanced computing systems will increasingly become part and parcel of a bench scientist's role.

Animal Sciences

Careers in animal sciences exist wherever animal testing of drug candidates is conducted. That covers a vast array of private and government laboratories. In the private sector, animal facilities supervisors, veterinarians, and lab assistants are responsible for acquiring, maintaining, and providing the animals needed for initial testing of drug candidates, when the drug's safety is determined.

Animal sciences positions usually have titles like veterinarian (vet), facility manager, lab assistant, and glasswasher. Of those, vets and facility managers are professional positions that require at least a college and/or professional degree. The others require no more than a high school diploma, and will not be elaborated upon here. All professional jobs need at least several years of experience to break in.

The Outlook for Laboratory Research Careers

Recruiters expect strong demand for candidates in bioinformatics, clinical research, and biomanufacturing in the next 10 years. As more drug candidates emerge from discovery research and enter clinical trials, the need for people to staff all levels of clinical trials becomes more urgent. That same trend will have a positive effect on manufacturing positions. As drug candidates emerge from clinical trials, they will need to go into production, hence the need for people with manufacturing skills. This means that for those preparing for a career in the industry, these fields are particularly open.

The picture is not quite as rosy for discovery research. Several recruiters note that, with the industry restructuring, "smaller companies are struggling; larger companies will be able to absorb people displaced from the smaller outfits that fold." Specifically, discovery research is likely to be hardest hit and "one of the areas of least growth in the current climate since the return on investment is the slowest," according to recruiters. For those wanting to pursue a career in discovery research, this situation makes it even more important – as we have mentioned throughout this volume – to describe the impact of your research on meeting milestones (and hence revenue payments) and other corporate goals.

Let's take a look at the story revealed in some hard data. According to a Department of Commerce study, between 2000-2002, the scientific part of the biotech workforce grew at an average annual rate of 12.3%, a figure that increases to 17.3% for small to mid-size companies. Be careful in interpreting this result, however. Whereas the percentage increase seems large, in fact, the greatest employment (in numbers of workers) comes from the large companies. R&D-focused computer jobs grew at a 21.8% average annual rate – a statistic that confirms the great demand for bioinformatics professionals. This is not surprising, since the field is less than a decade old and, as we pointed out, requires two sets of expertise. Scientific and laboratory technician employment grew at the next highest rate or 13.8%. Scientific and engineering employment grew at 10.8% and 10.7%, respectively. (Check out technology.gov for more details.)

Visit Vault at www.vault.com for insider company profiles, expert advice, career message boards, expert resume reviews, the Vault Job Board and more.

V/\ULT CAREER LIBRARY   **127**

Qualifications for Non-Lab Research Careers

CHAPTER 11

Engineering

Product/Process Engineering

Operations positions come into existence when a company has identified compounds that are commercially viable. As we have said, these jobs have a hands-on, practical engineering bent. In actual companies, the quality and validation functions are separated from the manufacturing function to ensure complete objectivity; we've grouped them here for clarity of presentation.

The product/process development group is where engineers scale up compound processes for mass production. Scaling up processes refer to the adjustments necessary to permit production of a formulation in commercial quantities. Specifically, this means that some components of a formulation may have to be substituted since they do not behave identically in large quantities as they do at the laboratory bench. Alternatively, different equipment – e.g., ovens – may have to be used to treat materials at larger scale. Optimizing manufacturing processes involves ensuring that the equipment and facilities used to manufacture biological materials are utilized as cost effectively as possible. Maximizing yields and plant utilization are of concern here. Finally, working with computerized instrumentation and micro-measurement equipment is also quite useful experience, since virtually all laboratory instruments contain computing power to ease crunching of generated data and since many procedures require the ability to measure minute quantities of matter. Special equipment is needed to measure quantities on the order of one-thousandth of a one-thousandth, or 10-6. (Note that the term "nanotechnology" refers to processes and reactions occurring on an even smaller scale – i.e., 10-9.)

Process/product development positions usually have titles like technician, associate, and supervisor. All positions require a BS/MS level of education in engineering and varying degrees of experience, preferably in a biopharmaceutical research and development environment. If you have a BS degree but no internship or co-op experience, breaking into an entry-level technician job will be tough. If you have an MS degree but no industry experience, you qualify for an associate job.

This picture, however, is not set in stone. With the appropriate internship, you can probably land a technician job. The size of the company and the demand in your specific geographic area will be factors in landing a job without experience. Here's a scenario of how that can happen. You live in one of the six states that have a strong biotech presence. Several products move into Phase III just around the time you graduate. Demand for process developers ticks up as companies look for people to help make more product available for the expanded Phase III trials. They can't skimp because this phase is the most expensive to set up and run; product has to be available for all enrolled patients. You then present yourself as an eager candidate.

If you want to target a technician job, be prepared to work under close supervision, as you will be implementing the development work defined by senior lab personnel. Technicians mix compounds, prepare test samples, operate and maintain instrumentation and computer equipment, and maintain lab records and inventory of materials.

Process/product development associates evaluate, improve, and figure out how to scale-up manufacturing processes. They handle small- to medium-scale production work, doing work with cell cultures, fermentation, protein purification, and protein separation using chromatography techniques. Associates also help out in maintaining production equipment.

Manufacturing engineering

Now suppose you've figured out how to scale up that cake to feed 80 and are now ready to go into production. So you can now produce one batch of cake to feed 80, but the company needs thousands of cakes. At this point, we're in the manufacturing environment. Manufacturing positions usually have titles like technician, associate, supervisor, manager, and director. All of them need BS degrees in engineering. Of those positions, only manufacturing technicians are entry-level jobs.

Manufacturing technicians assist in specific product-related operations relating to cell culture and fermentation. They operate and maintain production equipment, such as fermenters and bioreactors, and perform procedures, such as cell harvesting and separation. Manufacturing technicians weigh, measure, and check raw materials to assure the accuracy of weights of ingredients. They prepare media and mix buffer solutions, maintain records and assists with test procedures.

Manufacturing skills, like process development skills are likely to be at a premium in the next few years, since more and more products are emerging from clinical trials. "As products emerge from clinical trials and into actual production, biotech manufacturing employment at all levels is expected to increase, with experienced people able to command a premium," a biotech industry recruiter notes.

Environmental health and safety engineering

Environmental health and safety positions have titles like toxicologist and environmental engineer. Toxicologists design and implement toxicity sick (i.e., figure out what drug candidates make animals sick and determine to what degree they get sick) to support product registration requirements. They need to have at least an MS degree, although many companies prefer a Ph.D. Environmental engineers research, coordinate, implement, and manage environmental issues, including regular and hazardous waste disposal, air/water quality, pollution control, and land management. They need a BS in environmental, civil, or chemical engineering, although many companies prefer an MS. Neither position is available at an entry level.

Quality engineering

Since customers of your grandma's favorite cake would become unhappy if their cakes varied from batch to batch, you'll want to make sure that every batch is the same and that the recipe is followed to the letter each time you make a batch. Ensuring that consistency is the realm of the quality group. Most positions require at least a BS degree for entry-level professionals and an MS for managerial jobs. Quality positions have titles like quality assurance analyst, documentation specialist, quality assurance supervisor, quality assurance manager, and quality assurance director. Of these positions, only the QA qnalyst is an entry-level position after earning an undergraduate degree.

QA analysts conduct the more routine analyses and are considered entry-level professionals. They work on raw materials, in-process, and finished formulations, usually under close supervision and according to standard operating procedures (SOPs). To target a job as a QA Analyst, look toward earning a BS in microbiology, chemistry, or biochemistry. Depending on the demand in your area, you can break in without industry experience, but be sure you land that all-important internship, as many companies really prefer that you have at least some industry experience.

Visit Vault at **www.vault.com** for insider company profiles, expert advice, career message boards, expert resume reviews, the Vault Job Board and more.

VAULT CAREER LIBRARY   **131**

Validation

The validation group makes sure that things do what they're supposed to do. For example, DNA fingerprinting technology helps identify paternity cases. You want to be sure the procedure and the equipment used give you definitive results that yield a conclusion beyond a reasonable doubt. Positions are available for validation specialists and validation managers. Neither position is available at the entry level. Validation specialists develop and recommend strategies and design studies to validate systems, equipment, methods, and processes. You'll need to earn a BS in a scientific or engineering field, know about current industry practices and cGMP requirements, and have several years of experience to land one of these jobs.

Medical and Clinical Setting Careers

It is essential to ensure that the drug candidates – get tested on controlled human patient populations. This is the realm of clinical professionals. Larger companies have several distinct groups: clinical research, clinical data management, regulatory affairs, and medical affairs/drug information.

Clinical research group

The clinical research group is responsible for arranging and managing clinical trials, ensuring that FDA regulations are met and that the various clinical professionals needed to carry out clinical trials have the information they need to do their work smoothly and efficiently. The clinical research group has positions for clinical research associates (CRAs), clinical research managers, and biostatisticians. None of these positions are available at the entry level.

Clinical research associates (CRAs) are at the front lines of implementing and monitoring clinical trials and preparing regulatory report submissions to the FDA. They provide input in recruiting and hiring clinical data management personnel (e.g., investigators, contract researchers, other vendors), since teamwork and consistency is essential. CRAs usually require a BS in a scientific or health care field (e.g., nursing, pharmacy, physician's assistant) and several years of clinical research experience.

Biostatisticians ensure the statistical integrity, adequacy, and accuracy of the clinical studies and associated databases. They implement statistical analysis methodology; perform statistical programming, design, and analyses for clinical trial projects; and provide insight on data interpretation. Biostatisticians need at least an MS, though many companies prefer a Ph.D. and several years of experience.

Clinical data management group

The clinical data management group is in charge of collecting and processing the reams of data that the CRAs collect in clinical trials. Positions are available for clinical data associates, clinical data managers, programmer/analysts, and clinical database managers. All positions need a BS/MS degree and solid skills in using personal computers and software applications. Of these positions, only the clinical data associate is an entry-level job.

You may well wonder why entry-level credentials are acceptable for employers in this case but not for the CRAs. The distinction, if you haven't noticed already lies in the difference between working on people and working with data. CRAs help physicians actually administer drugs to patients, a task that requires training, practice, and general orientation to clinical settings. Clinical data associates do more of the hands-on work with clinical data, such as reviewing discrepancies and entering corrections in databases and assisting in creating final reports. The skills you develop in college — writing papers, working with data sets in quantitative courses and interpreting results — readily transfer to data-handling responsibilities. In addition to the hands-on work, clinical data associates also assist the managers who review the clinical trials site, supervise clinical investigators and ensure that good clinical practices (GCPs) are followed.

Regulatory affairs

Larger companies maintain a regulatory affairs group, whose mandate is to stay on top of any and all regulatory requirements. The group coordinates and prepares regulatory submissions to both the FDA and international regulations. All positions require at least a BS/MS degree. Positions are available for documentation associates/assistants, regulatory affairs associates, regulatory affairs managers, and regulatory affairs director. Of those positions, only the regulatory affairs associate is an entry-level job.

Regulatory affairs associates do most the hands-on work of the group. They prepare document packages, maintain files and archives, and provide reports and other documentation to other departments (e.g., manufacturing, QA/QC, medical affairs, and clinical research). Associates prepare outlines,

Visit Vault at **www.vault.com** for insider company profiles, expert advice, career message boards, expert resume reviews, the Vault Job Board and more.

VAULT CAREER LIBRARY   **133**

summaries, status reports, graphs, charts, tables, and slides for distribution and communication to other departments. They also assist in researching and analyzing regulatory information and ensuring compliance with product registration requirements.

Administrative and Support Functions

Finance group

The finance group is in charge of the numbers. Finance jobs in small, research-oriented biotech firms require very high degrees of experience. If you've got your eye on a finance job in the biotech industry, you'll need to set your sight on the larger companies. There, you are likely to find fully developed career tracks in finance.

The finance group usually has two tiers of positions. At the lower end, accounting and payroll clerks, who do routine calculations, check and verify postings, analyze accounts, and do other basic accounting functions. These positions do not require a college degree and are not considered professional level. At the other end are positions like accounting manager, director of finance, chief financial officer, and vice president of finance and administration. All of these positions require at least a BS in accounting or finance, preferably with either a CPA or MBA and varying numbers of years of experience. All of these positions require some experience in the field.

This odd-looking, two-tier track is characteristic of very small biotech companies. It makes sense when you consider that very senior people are needed to arrange the funding for a start-up or an early-stage venture. Funding activities require ongoing negotiations and presentations to venture capital and private equity groups, tasks that require depth and sophistication. Since these companies usually have very small numbers of employees, there are relatively few routine duties involved in getting payroll checks out and looking after company accounts. For those tasks, a simpler set of skills is acceptable and provides support for the senior manager. Larger companies populate the middle ranks with analyst positions and mid-level management positions, but these too require some industry exposure.

External relations group

Biotech companies employ any one of several types of external relations managers to deal with the public, investor community, and government. These jobs usually need a BS in English, journalism, public relations, or communications and several years of industry-specific experience, as well as oral and written communications skills. Positions have titles like public relations manager, investor relations manager, and government relations manager. All of these positions require some experience to break in.

Human resources group

The human resources (HR) group handles the "people aspect" of the company. We put that in quotes because several aspects of HR require expertise that is pretty far removed from the soft skills the term suggests. Benefits and compensation people need to understand salary structures, bonus plans, retirement plans, and the ever-changing, ever-challenging healthcare delivery plans. They need to be quantitative and very detail oriented. Compliance people, those who make sure the company hiring and firing procedures meet Federal labor laws need to be very comfortable reading legal documents – the laws themselves, case law rulings and interpretations, and pending legislation on prospective new laws. Recruiting and training are elements of HR that properly have a "people aspect." Positions are available for human resource representatives, human resource managers, and director of human resources. All positions require at least a BS degree, preferably in business, human resources, or psychology as well as varying degrees of experience. Specific experience in benefits administration, payroll, labor relations, training, and recruitment are particularly valuable. In addition, HR professionals also need strong communication skills and should demonstrate an understanding of the need for discretion in handling employee information. All of these positions require some experience to break in.

Information systems group

The information systems group helps keep the company's computer systems running. As we've noted previously, this group focuses on all departments, in contrast with the bioinformatics group, which works mainly with discovery researchers. Most companies require a BS in computer science and at least several years of industry-specific experience. Positions are available for analyst/programmers, systems analysts, and manager of information systems.

Visit Vault at **www.vault.com** for insider company profiles, expert advice, career message boards, expert resume reviews, the Vault Job Board and more.

VAULT CAREER LIBRARY   **135**

Analyst/programmers provide hands-on work in designing, developing, coding, testing, debugging, and documenting software applications. Systems analysts focus on the design, customization, and implementation of software systems. All of these positions require some experience to break in.

Legal group

The biotech industry employs several types of attorneys in its legal group, all of which need a JD degree and varying levels of experience. Patent and intellectual property (IP) attorneys prepare and prosecute patent applications. Labor/employment law attorneys provide counsel for all matters involving human and labor relations. Contract attorneys focus on preparing and modifying contracts, leases, non-standard agreements, etc.

Project Management

The work of the project management group is inherently inter-disciplinary. The group's mandate is to bring people of different parts of the company together to work toward the same goal. That seems simple enough, but when you consider that people in different functions are compensated on different performance criteria, you can begin to see why it takes special skill to get everyone pointed in the same direction. All positions require at least a BS degree. Positions usually have titles like project assistant, project manager, and director of project management

If you're training for a career in any of these areas, this section can feel like a real downer. However, keep in mind that the biotech industry is still relatively young and the total number of these support positions is less than that for discovery researchers. One way to break in is to target Big Pharma companies, which have very well developed support infrastructures. Another route is to target the top 10 biotechs, which, as we have said, are mid-cap pharmaceutical companies. Finally, stay abreast of the growth prospects of a company. Do they have a full product pipeline? Have recent FDA pronouncements been favorable? Do they have an organic growth strategy in addition to one by acquisition? If so, the company is likely to build up its corporate infrastructure, and that translates into more support function positions.

Sales and Marketing

Sales

Sales jobs for biotech products are generally different from traditional pharmaceutical sales in that they tend to be targeted at smaller populations, are much more expensive, have larger profit margins, and are part of vastly smaller sales forces. This means that fewer opportunities exist. Furthermore, the traditional sales rep calls on as many as eight to 10 physicians per day and has general knowledge of a disease condition and extensive knowledge of his/her company's product line. Since most biotech products are essentially specialty pharmaceuticals, their sales process is a bit different. The biotech sales rep is expected to have extensive knowledge of both the disease pathology and the product itself. And since targeted patient populations are quite small, the biotech sales rep often becomes an intrinsic part of the case management team, providing information not just to physicians, but also to other healthcare professionals (nurses, clinical social workers, therapists, etc.) who collaboratively contribute to the care of a patient with a rare genetic disease.

These conditions require that the sales rep already have a full orientation to the industry as well as have well-developed people skills. Sales positions require a BA/BS in a scientific discipline and some professional experience in biopharmaceuticals. Some people have MBAs, but this is not as big of a requirement in sales as it is in marketing. Other people enter sales from allied health fields, such as nursing, or from discovery research positions, mostly from those not requiring a Ph.D. Still others, and this is a relatively new development, have very high levels of education – often an MD – and serve as much as liaisons to medical specialists providing sophisticated product information on rare genetic diseases.

Sales positions usually have titles like sales associate, account executive and specialty representative and medical liaison officer. Biotech sales positions are not available at the entry level.

If you want to target a sales position, your best bet is to get an entry-level position at a company that sells conventional pharmaceuticals, then move to a specialty product line. That may or may not be with the same company. Many big pharma companies are snapping up biotechs to fill up their research pipelines and round out their product lines, so it is entirely conceivable that you can get both types of experience under the same roof. Still, industry

Visit Vault at **www.vault.com** for insider company profiles, expert advice, career message boards, expert resume reviews, the Vault Job Board and more.

VAULT CAREER LIBRARY   **137**

insiders confide that applicants should demonstrate at least a year of sales experience to break in.

Marketing

Marketing positions typically require an MBA, a BA/BS in economics, econometrics, statistics, or finance and varying degrees of professional experience in biopharmaceuticals. Positions usually have titles like marketing research analyst, product marketing manager, marketing manager, and vice president of marketing. A word about management jobs: Drugs are marketed by therapeutic area, such as oncology and cardiology. So, different marketing managers will be responsible for product lines in specific therapeutic areas. This practice is consistent in the marketing of both small molecules and biologics. It will be tough to break in at the BS level without any industry experience, although you might be able to land a job at the larger biotechs as a marketing research analyst. At the MBA level, an analyst position is accessible. Depending on whether you get experience between your BS and MBA, you might also be able to land a position as a product manager.

Marketing research analysts support marketing management by providing information and analysis using both qualitative and quantitative market research data. Analysts develop financial models, research market trends, awareness, adoption and attitudes of newly launched products and analyze data sets from providers, patients, and other groups. They also complete competitive strategy assessments and analyze targeted markets for feasibility, profitability, and strategic fit.

Business development

In the last decade, a new role has emerged within the sales and marketing area. Business development is part sales, part marketing, part diplomacy, part wheeling and dealing, part finance, and part strategy. And by the way, you have to understand the science well enough to be able to describe it on your feet after a hectic travel schedule to a potential partner. In a company's organization chart, positions in business development fall within the marketing box, which is why we are including it in this section. Smaller companies focused on discovery research often do not have marketing/sales groups. As companies grow and a product/service is refined enough to commercialize, marketing/sales becomes differentiated from the search and management of alliances; such groups usually operate under the business development umbrella.

Within business development, you'll find two distinct roles: new business development (or chasing after new customers, partners, etc.) and alliance management (or maintaining the relationships with the customers, partners, etc. already identified). According to a vice president of business development, "This differentiation is a sign of the evolution of the industry. In addition, business development activities can occur on both the buy and sell sides. You can be involved in either selling offerings or, alternatively, identifying and purchasing services or capabilities." He adds, "Although critical, it is often not a large department in most companies."

"Generally, biotech companies are dependent on a few bigger relationships instead of many small ones. As such, selling is very much about communicating competence and building trust for a long-term relationship, not just focusing on the best 'deal' for the immediate opportunity. It is not about the often stereotyped view of a pushy sales person," says the VP.

To be considered, you need an MBA and a BA/BS in a scientific discipline, plus various levels of professional experience, preferably in different functions throughout the the industry. All the majors of discovery research are acceptable. The main point here is not so much the specific knowledge base although that is in itself necessary – but rather the conceptual orientation and basic understanding of the language and methods used in biotechnology applications. Industry experience usually refers to companies actively engaged in producing or utilizing products produced by the biotech industry. This usually means Big Pharma, Big Biotech, or hospitals and other clinical settings. Positions usually have titles like research analyst, manager of corporate planning, and vice president of business development. With an MBA and a scientific undergraduate degree, it is possible to land an entry-level position as a research analyst. However, we need to hedge a bit here, as many companies prefer that you have some experience before getting hired. That can come from several sources, including strategy consulting, investment banking, or corporate partnering and deal making. You'll need to know due diligence, asset valuation, alliance integration, and portfolio management. Work in this function requires both strong analytical and excellent communication and organizational skills.

The biotech industry places a premium on being an insider because the nature of the work requires that business development people have a thorough understanding of the intellectual capital of the company – often, products must be sold before they even exist. In order to represent a small discovery

Visit Vault at **www.vault.com** for insider company profiles, expert advice, career message boards, expert resume reviews, the Vault Job Board and more.

VAULT CAREER LIBRARY   **139**

research oriented company properly, the "biz dev" people need to be able to understand the work of the scientists, determine the optimal alliance with a marketing partner, and close a deal profitably. The sheer breadth of this mandate suggests that this function attracts people from various paths. According to the VP, "typically, there is an underpinning of science somewhere in their background. Some people come in from the legal side, usually from having negotiated contracts. In business development, you see a convergence of three core elements: science, legal, and business. People develop business development careers in this industry coming from any of these disciplines."

The softer side of business development cannot be overestimated. "You spend a lot of time communicating. The most important key to success is perseverance. You have to have a willingness to find a way past challenges and hurdles that will arise. Then, there's great satisfaction when things happen. It takes self-discipline to achieve balance; time and priorities management are essential to making your life work," says the VP. Furthermore, "Success is not just signing a deal. Success comes longer term from what is produced. It takes effective management to make alliances work," he adds. "Although you have some control over outcomes, other factors are also outside your control, and that can be frustrating. Events such as budget cycles can cause delays in implementing a deal. You have to be more proactive than reactive and to manage your time and priorities." Sometimes, "some opportunities don't happen that should happen, and that can be disappointing."

Resumes and Interviews

CHAPTER 12

Basic Resume Advice

Recent graduates should emphasize educational achievements by placing that section first on the resume, whereas experienced professionals usually place their experience first and education last on their resumes. Whatever format you choose, remember that, above all, your resume is a tool to help you land an interview. The resume should be as specific as possible to the job you are targeting. They should also be impeccably presented, easy to scan and clear in specifying achievements.

A word of caution: Many scientific resumes contain highly specialized terminology. When choosing what to include in your resume, if you have any doubt that the hiring manager might not understand or recognize an acronym or other term, either leave it out or spell it out. A good rule of thumb is to include standard terminology in the field, but spell out acronyms that are specific to a company and may not be familiar to people outside the company.

If you have biotech experience, remember to note both what you did (your actions) and what you accomplished (the results achieved) in several concisely written bullets that can be scanned quickly by a hiring manager. Progress is easy to quantify if you work in sales/marketing (exceeded sales goals by 5 percent; increased market share by 12 percent), but can be less clearcut if you work in discovery research, for example. In such cases, think about how your performance increased efficiency, met milestones (which often have revenue payments attached to them), or created new and promising avenues of investigation. In research, for example, focus on times when you contributed an idea that was adopted by the group or if you figured out a way to do procedures a little more efficiently. In the venture capital-funded biotech world, time is money and scientists are expected to have something to show for the investor dollars they have been given.

Visit Vault at www.vault.com for insider company profiles, expert advice, career message boards, expert resume reviews, the Vault Job Board and more.

VAULT CAREER LIBRARY   141

Recent Graduate Resume

PETER DOE, PH.D.
1 Devonshire Place, Apt 3003, Boston, MA 02109
(617) 320-8789 (mobile)
pdoe@evelexa.com

EDUCATION

HARVARD UNIVERSITY, GRADUATE SCHOOL OF ARTS & SCIENCES Boston, MA
Doctor of Philosophy, Virology   January 2001
• Thesis: CD4-Independent Replication of a CCR5-Using HIV-1 Primary Isolate.

CORNELL UNIVERSITY   Ithaca, NY
Bachelor of Arts, Biology   May 1997
• Honors Thesis: Non-cytolytic release of Canine Parvovirus. Advisor: Dr. Colin Parrish

EXPERIENCE

RA CAPITAL ASSOCIATES (www.racap.com)   Cambridge, MA
Director   June 2001 -
• Evaluate all investment opportunities, ranging from biotechnology startups to public
  companies.
• Assist Managing Director Richard Aldrich, former CBO of Vertex Pharmaceuticals, on
  business development and strategy-related advisory projects.

EVELEXA BIORESOURCES (www.evelexa.com) – 4500+ members   Boston, MA
Founder, Director   January 2001 –
• Developed educational web site that offers free business information related to starting
  biotech companies.
• Author an article each month for e-mail distribution to members.
• Members may download a free copy of the Entrepreneur's Guide to a Biotech Startup

INDEPENDENT CONSULTING   Boston, MA
                                                                January 2001 -

• Pearlacon, Inc. Proteomics start-up
  Proposed specifications for prototype drug-screening platform.
• Eleusis Biomedical, Inc. Diagnostics start-up.
  Helped raise $1.4M of a $4.5M A round.
• Global Prior Art, Inc. www.globalpriorart.com. Intellectual property consulting firm.
  Developed and executed business and marketing strategy targeting biotech community.

PUBLICATIONS

ENTREPRENEUR'S GUIDE TO A BIOTECH START-UP. THIRD EDITION. 2002
Author/Editor
• A 100+ page guide for biotech entrepreneurs. Background research included interviews with
  attorneys, venture capitalists, entrepreneurs, scientists, angel investors, technology transfer
  specialists, and others. The third and prior editions have been available for free download as
  of March, 2001 at www.evelexa.com

ADDITIONAL

• Co-founder of BiotechTuesday (www.biotechtuesday.com), Boston networking event series.
  1,700+ members
• Founded Harvard Biotechnology Club in 1999. (www.thebiotechclub.org). 4,000+ members
• Enjoy snowboarding, sailing, and travel.

Experienced Professional Resume

JANE SMILES

123 Hopalong Way
Petaluma, CA 33333
(555) 555-1111
smiles@yahoo.com

SUMMARY

Ph.D. research scientist with experience in putting chemical engineering and biology principles to work to substantially improve processes in cell therapy, tissue engineering, and protein production. Track record of promptly and thoroughly designing and executing programs that led to successes in research, development, validation, quality control, and regulatory affairs aspects of GMP-compliant processes. Demonstrated in-depth knowledge of statistical hypothesis testing, automated data acquisition, and control and database design and programming to meet needs of internal and external clients. Developed and motivated interdisciplinary teams to encourage group learning and convert individual skills to group results.

EDUCATION

Ph.D., Chemical Engineering, California Institute of Technology, Menlo Park, CA 1991
BS, Biology and Chemical Engineering, Carnegie-Mellon, Pittsburgh, PA 1986

PROFESSIONAL EXPERIENCE

CRICK CORPORATION
Director, Process Development

Responsible for development and manufacturing efforts in cell therapy products targeted to reconstitute the human immune system and support diabetic patients.

- Implemented manufacturing process for cell therapy product involving expanded primary human cells. Product has been approved by U.S. FDA for use in human clinical trials.
- Oversaw research on process improvements for product.
- Guided preclinical development efforts on novel implantable stem cell therapy based on expanding primary human cells. Translated research, bench-scale processes into scalable cell manufacturing processes.
- Contributed research data and other technical information to FDA submissions. Managed all manufacturing SOPs and batch records for clinical production. Implemented statistical process control of manufacturing runs to monitor stability of process and evaluate effect of process changes or vendor or lot changes in raw materials.
- Wrote functional specification for overall laboratory relational database management system.
- Directed all work of 10-person group, including Ph.D.-level scientists, MS-level senior research associates, and additional research associates. Defined workplans, administered performance reviews and salary actions. Recruited and hired group members at all levels.

ANONOMATICS
Director, Diagnostic Bioengineering

Responsible for all clinical trial activities of company. Responsible for all "wet lab" (analytical) functions of company.

- Authored protocols for and supervised conduct of a total of five human clinical trials: three human clinical trials on noninvasive glucose monitoring through ultrasound-

Visit Vault at **www.vault.com** for insider company profiles, expert advice, career message boards, expert resume reviews, the Vault Job Board and more.

V/\ULT CAREER LIBRARY   **143**

pretreated skin, and two human clinical trials on drug delivery through ultrasound-pretreated skin. Designed and wrote study protocols, received approval from external institutional review boards, designed case report forms, designed and implemented relational study databases in Microsoft Access, audited data, and wrote final reports. Authored manuscript on trial results.

- Prepared and delivered sections of investor presentations on company technology.
- Conducted animal studies. Designed study protocols, received approval from institutional animal care and use committee, and executed protocols.
- Conducted in-house laboratory studies and invented processes and data analysis techniques leading to three active patent applications.
- Directed work of one MS chemist in transdermal drug delivery through pretreated skin. This work assessed enhancement in drug delivery achieved by ultrasound pretreatment for several classes of compounds.
- Directed work of four BS analysts in performing HPLC analyses, protein electrophoresis, ELISAs, and other laboratory tasks. Recruited and hired analysts, and completed performance reviews and salary actions.

SUPRACELLS
Associate Director, Engineering

Responsible for developing and implementing an annual R&D Engineering operational budget of approximately $300,000 and for directing and carrying out engineering development program for two bioartificial organs. One product was in FDA-approved pivotal clinical trials. The other product was approved to enter clinical trials.

- Developed and implemented laboratory and manufacturing processes consistent with GMP and GLP requirements. Wrote, reviewed, and maintained SOPs for these processes.
- Performed product safety testing to international, European, and U.S. guidelines.
- Conducted in vitro metabolic studies to mimic the intended action of bioartificial organs. Monitored oxygen consumption, cell viability, and metabolism of marker compounds to support efforts in research, product and process development, quality control, and regulatory affairs. Ensured that laboratory studies operated as closely as possible to clinical use conditions, thus maximizing agreement between laboratory and clinical data.
- Represented company in tissue-engineered medical products standards initiative of the American Society for Testing and Materials, in collaboration with FDA Center for Devices and Radiological Health.
- Produced data, including GLP validation package, demonstrating superiority of company's bioreactor over previously used bioreactor from an outside vendor. FDA approved the new device for use in clinical trials. Device has performed in patients as predicted.

PETROFUN, INC.
Senior Research Engineer
Research Engineer

Responsible for conducting laboratory research on bioreactor systems and for developing novel quality control procedures for medical devices.

- Produced various monoclonal antibodies at gram-per-day scale for internal projects.
- Specified hardware and designed software for a computerized dialyzer test system. Installed four of these systems in three company laboratories in two states, on time, within budget, and with performance that exceeded design specifications independent of location or operator.
- Formulated and tested cell culture media and additives to maximize product formation, secretion, purity, and yield. Reduced medium consumption of cells fourfold over previous company experience without reducing antibody production rates. Met customer request for better-defined medium composition and reduced costs. Obtained patent on this medium.
- Implemented testing program to characterize behavior of developmental medical device materials on repeated exposure to sterilizing agents. Identified key performance parameters and monitored those parameters as a function of reuse cycle number. Information from these tests created a more robust device and provided data for product labeling claims.

Preparing for the Interview

Prepare for your interviews by thinking through two sets of issues: first, about your own achievements and goals, and second, about the potential employer.

In thinking about your experience, consider the work and projects you have completed in your career. Determine your contribution to the projects and practice describing your contributions succinctly. Next, be sure you understand what the project produced and be prepared to explain that to the hiring manager. Remember that you are likely to be more expert than the hiring manager on your former work projects, so be sure that your story defines the objectives of the project, its team structure, your roles and responsibilities, and the key outcomes of the project in general and your specific achievements.

Interviewing tips

These tips apply to any interview you do:

- Be on time.
- Be focused and motivated but relaxed.
- Make steady eye contact.
- Carry a portfolio only (or a portfolio and purse for women).
- Respond to the interviewer's greeting by repeating his/her name. (e.g., "Good Morning, Mary, I'm glad to meet you.")
- Familiarize yourself with the company's products, recent press releases, history, and management structure.
- Review recent annual reports and 10K filings to understand the company's financial status
- Identify the functional area you are interested in and are applying for.
- Ask informed questions. (e.g., "Can you tell me a bit about how the company is addressing the pricing challenges facing the pharmaceutical industry?")
- Carry extra copies of your resume.
- Dress in conservative styles and colors. It's hard to go wrong with black, navy, or gray.
- Be prepared to describe specific examples from past work experiences, as well as what you learned from them.
- Inquire about next steps in the hiring process at the conclusion of the interview.

Visit Vault at **www.vault.com** for insider company profiles, expert advice, career message boards, expert resume reviews, the Vault Job Board and more.

VAULT CAREER LIBRARY   **145**

Avoid:

- Cerebral or long-winded answers to questions. Don't ramble.
- Wearing perfumes or colognes or any scent that is obvious.
- Asking questions that reveal ignorance of basic facts about the employer.
- Taking too many notes, so that you break eye contact for significant bits of time (i.e., more than a few seconds per note).
- Asking the interviewer to evaluate you at the end of the interview.
- Giving a business card. The interviewer has your resume and will contact you again if the company is interested in you. However, you should ask for a copy of your interviewer's business card.

After the interview:

- Avoid contacting the interviewer immediately afterward by phone. This smacks of desperation and your interviewer may feel harassed. Wait two weeks to follow up.
- Send a thank you note.

A Recruiter's Perspective on Interviews

"Interviews are an exercise in give and take," says a top biotech recruiter. "There's a natural fear at the prospect of being interviewed. But getting prepared is important. For most candidates, preparation boosts confidence. Every once in a while, we'll get someone who is overconfident, and we have to bring him down a bit."

Generally, there are three types of interviews. In the first type, "the interviewer begins by asking general questions to get the candidate to talk about himself first. The best preparation for this type of interview is to write out a synopsis of the interview – about five minutes – get in front of a significant other or a mirror and practice what you're going to say. Your job is to sell yourself and present your product – you – in the best way." Also, "Be sure to focus your presentation on the skills that match the skill set the hiring company is looking for."

In the second type, "the interviewer talks a lot about the position and gives little opportunity to the candidate to talk about himself. In that case, the candidate needs to turn the discussion around to present their skill set."

It's also important not to lose confidence when the interviewer suddenly poses a negative question or comment, such as "I really don't think that this is the right position for you" or "You don't seem to have the right experience for this job." A senior recruiter notes, "Many times, these types of questions are simply a test to see how the candidate will react in a difficult situation. The candidate can respond as follows, 'I'm surprised you feel that way. Didn't we discuss that what you are looking for is a candidate who [give details]' or 'Perhaps I didn't explain myself clearly before, but when I worked at XYZ Corp. I [give details].' The candidate can then go into an explanation of what they did that directly relates to the job."

"The third type of interview is a collaborative give and take – a sort of Q and A session. The case interview is an example. The best preparation for case interviews is to practice solving case problems with a friend in a simulated interview situation." The recruiter concludes that, "In all cases, becoming confident is largely a matter of being prepared."

Sample Interview Questions

Discovery Research

The following sample interview questions and answers are for the types of questions you should expect during an interview for a research associate position.

1. What technique is used to measure the number of copies of a gene or an RNA molecule in human tissues?
PCR or polymerase chain reaction in real time, as opposed to the conventional method, because the number of copies of the target molecule can be monitored for each PCR cycle.

2. What are the limitations of blotting techniques and what alternatives can you suggest?
The major limitation of blotting procedures is the length of time needed and the fact that they can accommodate only one probe at a time. DNA microchip technology permits the analysis of thousands of genes at the same time. DNA molecules are attached to the wafers in an organized array and are called the probes. DNA molecules taken from tissues are hybridized to the chips and are called targets, which are labeled with fluorescent light. The probes that

Visit Vault at **www.vault.com** for insider company profiles, expert advice, career message boards, expert resume reviews, the Vault Job Board and more.

VAULT CAREER LIBRARY **147**

have hybridized to the fluorescent targets are then identified by fluorescence microscopy."

3. As you probably know, much biotech research is funded by private investors through venture capital firms. Do you think your role can contribute to the economic success of the research group, and if so, how?
I believe everyone working for a company can contribute to the organization's economic success. Although the position I am applying for is at the entry-level, I understand that doing my work efficiently will prevent delays, which have a negative impact on the group's productivity. As I learned in my internship, getting clear direction early and proactively helps me stay on track. Note: The best candidates will be able to articulate a coherent answer to this question.

Bioinformatics

The following sample interview questions and answers are for the types of questions you should expect during an interview for a bioinformatics analyst/programmer position position.

1. Tell me about the different kinds of DNA sequences.
There are three kinds of DNA sequences. Genomic DNA comes from the genome and includes both genes and extragenic material. cDNA is reverse transcribed from mRNA and corresponds only to the expressed parts of the genome. Recombinant DNA is man-made and is composed of artificial DNA.

2. If you had 1,500 base pair pieces of random DNA and you wanted to know how many of them had homology to known genes, what would you do to determine that?
I would use a BLASTX search against a known protein database – such as MCBI's NR database. I would then sort them to determine how many were unique.

3. What else would you do?
Start over. Do a sequence assembly using programs such as FRAP or CAP3. Then do a BLASTX against NR and I would do an open reading frame search against the contigs (the assembled pieces of fragments).

Process/product development engineering

The following sample interview questions and answers are for the types of questions you should expect during an interview for a process/product development technician position.

1. You're probably aware that your responsibilities will include maintaining records. Give me some idea of why this task is important.
There are several important reasons to maintain meticulous lab records. The company has to comply with regulatory requirements for GMPs, or good manufacturing practices. If the FDA finds out that there was a breakdown in compliance, the product submitted for clinical trials will vary from batch to batch and the outcome of the trials will be put into question. In addition, such a situation will be costly in time and money, as the trials will be delayed and tests have to be redone. Finally, the company's reputation will be adversely affected and that's bad for everyone connected with the product and the company.

2. A lot of process development work is time-sensitive and requires that you get raw materials from others, do your work and make the proteins you produce available to the clinical trials group within a specified time frame. How well do you think you can work under these constraints?
I'm generally well organized and able to budget my time well. It was very important to develop these skills since I worked all during college. The important thing is to understand your priorities. I would look to my supervisor to set them and get clarification as situations change from day to day. There are, however, always times when things get really intense. For those days, it's best to stay really focused, be as productive as possible, and keep your sense of humor.

The following sample interview questions and answers are for the types of questions you should expect during an interview for a process/product development associate position.

1. What kinds of problems do you sometimes encounter with separation procedures in high-pressure liquid chromatography?
In HPLC, you want to make sure you have a clean separation of components in the mixture you're trying to separate, so that you don't get overlapping bands. With a clean separation, you can then determine the concentration of each component more precisely.

Visit Vault at **www.vault.com** for insider company profiles, expert advice, career message boards, expert resume reviews, the Vault Job Board and more.

VAULT CAREER LIBRARY   **149**

2. Suppose you're really pressed for time and you have a technician do some routine maintenance on an instrument needed by the senior scientist. How might you do that comfortably?

First, I'd locate the SOP, the standard operating procedure for maintenance, and make sure the tech reads through it and understands it. Next, I'll tell him that, although I'll be busy, I'll still have time to answer a question, should one come up. Finally, I'll tell him I'll check in on him when he's done and make sure the instrument is ready to be used. That way, he'll feel motivated to learn something new but also realize he's covered.

Manufacturing engineering

The following sample interview questions and answers are for the types of questions you should expect during an interview for a manufacturing technician position.

1. What is the difference between, GMP, GLP, cGMP and why are they important?

All of these terms refer to different sets of practices that should be followed by the facility – whether a manufacturing facility or a development laboratory – to ensure that the products produced are of consistent and high quality from batch to batch. GMP refers to 'good manufacturing practices,' GLP refers to 'good laboratory practices,' and cGMP refers to 'current good medical practices.' The last term is applied in clinical trial settings.

2. How is the manufacturing of a biologic similar to or different from that for a conventional drug?

Traditional pharmaceutical companies produce synthetic chemicals that are biologically active. These are considered "small molecules" relative to proteins – one of the main products produced by biotech companies. Making small molecules is relatively less complex and less expensive than making proteins or biologics because biologics originate from animals or cells, which need to be housed in special facilities.

Quality engineering

The following sample interview questions and answers are for the types of questions you should expect during an interview for a QA analyst position.

1. Give me some examples of tools you can use to implement QA procedures.

Many tools are available, and the best depends on the specific procedure to be carried out. Generally, templates, forms, checklists, and SOPs are the most common tools used in implementing QA best practices.

2. Tell me more about SOPs – what are they and why are they necessary?

SOPs stands for standard operating procedures. They are developed to ensure that the steps taken in the manufacture of a product are exactly the same from batch to batch. That's very important for consistent quality. It is also important to meet regulatory requirements. SOPs are continually updated, as more efficient processes are identified. Then, that can become the new standard.

Clinical data management

The following sample interview questions and answers are for the types of questions you should expect during an interview for a clinical data associate position.

1. What attracts you to working with clinical data?

I'm looking forward to working with clinical data because I'm interested in seeing how a drug impacts people. I'm also detail-oriented and meticulous and enjoy looking at data sets to see if I can detect trends and patterns.

2. How do you think you can contribute to GCPs in your prospective position?

It's very important for everyone involved in clinical trials to ensure that best practices are followed. Good Clinical Practices are a set of protocols that clinical researchers need to follow to ensure the clinical trial is conducted properly. If these are not followed, the data generated will be questioned. I can do my part by helping ensure that the data that gets into the database is as the physician intended it.

3. How would you do that?

By proactively contacting the manager if I see a problem or by being alert to entries that seem really out of whack with what most patients are recording – say, a drug's reaction increases blood pressure 10% in most patients. If I see an entry that shows a drop of 20 or 30%, I might question it.

Visit Vault at www.vault.com for insider company profiles, expert advice, career message boards, expert resume reviews, the Vault Job Board and more.

VAULT CAREER LIBRARY   **151**

Regulatory affairs

The following sample interview questions and answers are for the types of questions you should expect during an interview for a regulatory affairs position.

1. Give me some examples of common regulatory submissions required of companies in approving new drugs and medical devices.
In approving new drugs, companies have to submit an NDA or New Drug Application. In approving medical devices, companies have to submit an IND or Investigational New Device application.

2. What about if we decide to license our technology?
In that case, you would have to submit a BLA or Biological Licensing Application.

Sales and marketing

The following sample interview questions and answers are for the types of questions you should expect during an interview for a marketing research analyst position.

1. Supposing you are asked to do market research for a new biologic targeted to treat a rare genetic disease with a U.S.-based patient population of approximately 5,000. How would you perform market research for this prospective new product?
Because the patient population is small, it is possible to do both quantitative and qualitative market research. I would first gather all the hard information available and get a sense of the distribution of patients in different geographies, the disease's rate of growth, its relative acuteness, and what health insurance carriers are currently covering. But I would also survey the medical specialists treating the patients as well as other members of the case team. From these comments, we can add insight to the quantitative data on how well the proposed new drug is being accepted.

2. Do you think genomic technology will impact your work as an analyst?
Yes, I do. Genomic technology will help identify small subsets of very large patient populations that experience the adverse effects that accompany any drug product. That means those populations can be identified and separated out. Instead of one big blockbuster, companies will have to produce several products tailored for specific subsets of patients. Market research will have to be performed on each set to identify their demographics and psychographics, geographies, and economics. Although that sounds more

complicated, it is also more exciting since medicine will be more customized to people's individual needs.

3. Can you identify some issues that affect the global marketing of conventional drugs and biologics?

Having consistent regulations in the major international markets – Europe and Japan – will certainly be a step forward. In other parts of the world, especially Asia and China, we need stronger intellectual property protection laws as an incentive to service those markets. Lastly, with price discrimination becoming more transparent, it's going to be increasingly tougher to charge different prices in different regions. All of these factors affect the marketing of drugs and biologics.

The following sample interview questions and answers are for the types of questions you should expect during an interview for a business development research analyst position.

1. Can you give me an example of a project you were involved with that illustrates your interest and skills in bringing people together?

I was the founder of the biotechnology club at my college. Although several other people co-founded the group, it was created at my initiative. We set up seminars where I got several key people in the industry to come speak to us on hot topics in the industry – like the agricultural biotech controversy and the ethical dimensions of stem cell research. The biotech club also sponsored a career fair, where we got over 100 students, soon to graduate, connected with over a dozen companies. I personally approached about half of those companies. I feel really proud about my contribution to this project.

2. How would you value a biotech company as opposed to a consumer products company?

Most companies are valued based on their growth prospects. That's what determines their stock price and overall dollar value, when they are sold. Biotech companies, as are other pharmaceutical companies, are valued based on the perceived quality of the products in their pipelines. That's what determines if they are going to have sustainable revenues and earnings. It's also why so many analysts on The Street pay such close attention to FDA pronouncements.

3. What kinds of metrics would you gauge to determine the financial, strategic, and operational health of a prospective alliance partner?

Several metrics are available in each sector you mention. To gauge the financial health of a prospective partner, I would look at product sales growth or I might look at whether they've met their milestones. To gauge strategic health, I'd consider their market share growth or, how well their customers have access to the company. For operational health, I'd again look to see whether they've met their milestones, how well they make decisions as gauged by the rating we give them, and how quickly they resolve conflicts. Good evaluations in these areas suggest that the prospective alliance will be viable for both parties.

APPENDIX

Biotech Glossary

Action letter: An FDA communication that informs an NDA or BLA sponsor that a decision has been made on the product. A letter of approval means that a product can be marketed.

Agonist: A drug that promotes certain kinds of cellular activity by binding to a cell's receptor.

Amino acids: The basic building blocks of protein, of which 22 are known. The nine "essential" amino acids cannot be synthesized by the body and must be obtained through the diet; the body can produce the other 13 "non-essential" amino acids.

Amplification: The process of increasing the number of copies of a particular gene or chromosomal sequence.

Antagonist: A drug that prevents certain types of cellular reactions by blocking other substances from binding to a cell's receptor.

Antibody: A protein produced by certain types of white blood cells to deactivate foreign proteins.

Antigen: Any substance that induces the body's immune response system via a specific antibody when it is introduced into the body.

Antisense: A drug that is the complementary image of a small segment of messenger RNA (mRNA), the substance that carries instructions from a cell's genes to its protein-making machinery. The drug is designed to bind to the mRNA strand, keeping it from transmitting its instructions to the cell and inhibiting the production of an unwanted protein. Antisense technology is used to selectively turn off production of certain proteins.

Assay: A test or technique that measures a biological response.

Autoimmune disease: A condition such as multiple sclerosis where the body produces antibodies against its own tissues.

Bioavailability: The percentage of a drug's active ingredient that reaches a patient's bloodstream and body tissues.

Biochip: A miniaturized test, usually slides or chips etched with genetic information, used by researchers to analyze DNA sequences, ascertain gene or protein expression, or detect single nucleotide polymorphisms (SNPs). Also known as microarrays or gene chips.

Bioinformatics: A system whereby biological information is collected, stored, accessed, and analyzed via information technology and other related electronic media. Bioinformatics is an important tool in genomics research since this type of research generates large complex data sets.

Biologicals (biologics, biologic drugs): Medicinal preparations made from living organisms or their byproducts (e.g., vaccines, antigens, serums, and plasmas).

Biologics license application (BLA): The formal filing that drug manufacturers submit to the FDA for approval to market new biologic-based drugs, which contains clinical evidence of the compound's safety and efficacy.

Biotechnology: The use of biological processes to solve human health, agricultural, and industrial problems and to commercialize useful products.

BLAST: Basic Local Alignment Search Tool used in bioinformatics. A database program used to search for similarities in DNA sequences.

Breakthrough drug: A compound whose mechanism of action is significantly different from that of existing drugs, representing a major therapeutic advance.

cGMP: Current good medical practices.

Chemotherapy drugs: Drugs used to treat cancers.

Chromosomes: Microscopic, threadlike components in the nucleus of a cell that carry hereditary information in the form of genes.

Clinical trials or clinical studies: Tests in which experimental drugs are administered to humans to determine their safety and efficacy. They routinely involve the use of a placebo group that is given an inactive substance that looks like the test product.

Clone: A group of identical genes, cells, or organisms derived from a single ancestor.

Clotting factors: Proteins involved in the normal clotting of blood.

Colony-stimulating factors: Proteins responsible for controlling the production of white blood cells.

Combinatorial chemistry: A technique to generate and screen up to millions of molecules with similar structure in order to find those with desired properties.

Combination therapy: The use of two or more drugs that, when taken together, have greater therapeutic power in treating illness and diseases than when either is used alone.

Copyrights: Form of legal protection of publishable works, such as books, articles, music, and virtually anything that is written by an author, including source code for software.

Codons: A set of three nucleotide bases in a DNA or RNA sequence, which together code for a specific amino acid.

Contigs: Common term in bioinformatics. Refers to groups of cloned DNA sequences that represent overlapping segments of a genome that are assembled together into one contiguous sequence.

Cross-licensing: Legal, contractual agreement between two firms with similar, possibly competing technologies which seeks to clarify who is to profit from the technology and limit legal action.

Deoxyribonucleic acid (DNA): The basic molecule that contains genetic information for most living systems. The DNA molecule consists of four nucleotide bases (adenine, cytosine, guanine, and thymine) and a sugar-phosphate frame arranged in two connected strands forming a double helix.

Diagnostics: A drug that is used to help diagnose a medical condition or disease. Monoclonal antibodies and DNA probes are useful diagnostics.

Employment agreement: A formal contract between an employer and a prospective employee specifying the terms of employment at the company.

Enzyme: Protein that controls chemical reactions in the body.

Expression: Manifestation of a characteristic exhibited by a gene. In biotechnology, the term means the production of a protein by a gene that has been inserted into a new host organism.

GLP: Good laboratory practices.

Gene: The basic determinant of heredity, genes are chromosomal segments that direct the syntheses of proteins and conduct other molecular regulatory functions.

Gene sequencing: A scientific technique whereby DNA strands are decoded in order to quantify the exact order of DNA's four nucleotides, A, C, T, and G. This method allows scientists to analyze the sequence of strands and identify specific genes embedded in DNA.

Visit Vault at **www.vault.com** for insider company profiles, expert advice, career message boards, expert resume reviews, the Vault Job Board and more.

V/\ULT CAREER LIBRARY   **159**

Gene therapy: The introduction of specific genes into a patient's body to replace defective ones or to suppress the action of a harmful one.

Genome: The total complement of genetic material in a cell, comprising the entire chromosomal set found in each nucleus of a given species.

Genomics: The study of genes and their functions, including mapping genes within the genome, identifying their nucleic acid structures, and investigating their functions.

GMP: good manufacturing practices.

Growth factors: Proteins responsible for regulating cell proliferation, function, and differentiation.

Freedom-to-operate: A company's ability to use and commercialize its own technology.

Functional genomics: The study of what a gene does, how it is regulated and how it interacts with other genes.

Human growth hormone: Pituitary hormone that stimulates the growth of long bones in pre-pubertal children.

Immunomodulator: A drug that attempts to modify the immune system.

Intellectual property (IP): The patents, trademarks, trade secrets, process innovation, know-how, and any other creative capital owned by a company. Intellectual property is often at the heart of a biotech company, and it is essential that the founders understand and document the IP they bring with them.

Interferon: A glycoprotein, produced naturally by cells, which interferes with a virus' ability to reproduce after it invades the body. Interferon may curtail the spread of certain types of cancer.

Interleukin: An endogenous substance that stimulates the production of different types of white blood cells or leukocytes.

Investigational new drug (IND): Regulatory classification of an experimental new compound that has successfully completed animal studies and has been approved by the FDA to proceed to human trials.

Joint venture: A type of deal between two companies whereby a third entity is created; often, joint ventures are nothing but paper companies in which each partner owns a portion of the profits and losses that result from the collaboration.

Licensing: A grant or permission needed to legalize use of a product, application of a process, exercising a right, etc. Under the Bayh-Dole Act, universities must transfer technology to industry – via technology licensing offices – so that government-sponsored research can be commercialized, and thus, benefit the public.

Macrophage: A type of white blood cell involved in the production of interleukin 1. These substances are being studied as potential anticancer therapies.

Managed care: A supervised system of financing and providing healthcare services for a defined population group. Preferred provider organizations (PPOs) and health maintenance organizations (HMOs) are currently the most popular forms of managed care.

Microarray: Miniature device – often a glass slide – that contains hundreds or thousands of different molecules that have been immobilized into a regular pattern. DNA microarrays are used for high-throughput genotyping; protein microarrays are used for detecting protein interactions.

Monoclonal antibodies: Large protein molecules produced by white blood cells, which seek out and destroy harmful foreign substances.

mRNA: Messenger RNA is a copy of DNA that is used to construct proteins from amino acids. By "copying" the genetic code into a second molecule and using it to do the heavy lifting of protein building, nature has found a way to protect the original code from wear and tear.

New drug application (NDA): The formal regulatory filing submission that drugmakers submit to the FDA for approval to market new chemical-based drugs. The NDA must include all relevant clinical data and information that a sponsor has collected during the product's research and development regarding the product's safety and efficacy. NDAs are extensive documents that have highly specific requirements for content and format.

Nucleic acid testing (NAT): A method of biological screening and diagnostic testing that entails amplifying DNA and RNA to identify diseases and infections. NAT is more accurate and faster than more traditional screens and is being used to test blood supplies for HIV and hepatitis infection.

Non-disclosure agreements (NDAs): A contract often used by information technology and biotech companies to protect the confidentiality of unreleased products and other sensitive information. In addition to specifying the nature of confidential information, NDAs also define the period of confidentiality, exceptions to the agreement, and terms of injunctive relief.

Visit Vault at **www.vault.com** for insider company profiles, expert advice, career message boards, expert resume reviews, the Vault Job Board and more.

VAULT CAREER LIBRARY   **161**

Orphan drug: A drug designed to treat a rare disease afflicting a relatively small patient population (currently fewer than 200,000 cases). The U.S. government gives drugmakers special incentives to encourage the development of such drugs.

Partnership: An organization of two or more persons or entities that pool resources and divide profits and losses. Partnership agreements may be formed with larger pharmaceutical companies whereby the biotech's product pipeline is its main asset base and the pharmaceutical's marketing and distribution prowess provide a logical pooling of expertise and resources.

Patent: An exclusive right given to an inventor by the U.S. government to prevent anyone from making, using, or selling a patented process or invention in the U.S. The patent protection period is 20 years for most patents, after which the knowledge disclosed in the patent application becomes part of the public domain. To be patentable, an invention must be useful, novel, and non-obvious.

Pharmacogenomics: The study of how an individual's genetic composition affects the response to drugs. It combines traditional pharmaceutical sciences such as biochemistry with the knowledge of genes, proteins, and single nucleotide polymorphisms.

Pharmacokinetics: Analysis of a drug's absorption and distribution in the body, its chemical changes in the body, and how it is stored and eliminated from the body.

Polymerase chain reaction (PCR): A scientific technique that uses special reagents and polymerase enzymes to amplify a specific fragment of DNA into larger quantities. PCR is used in a variety of genetic analysis settings, such as matching a DNA sample with a particular person or detecting infections.

Pre-money valuation: Value of a company before financing, often based on subjective assessments, such as quality of technology, business model, risk assessment, etc.

Priority review: An investigational drug receiving this status from the FDA will be reviewed by the agency within six months of its BLA or NDA submission.

Prodrug: An inactive compound that converts to an active agent through contact with a specific enzyme.

Proteome: The set of all proteins expressed by a genome.

Proteomics: The study of encoded proteins and their function, with an emphasis on the role that proteins may play in the development of disease.

Rational drug design: An approach to designing drugs wherein the known three-dimensional structure of a molecule – often a protein – is used to create a drug that will bind to it.

Recombinant DNA technology: The process of creating new DNA by combining components of DNA from different organisms. Usually, the new DNA is then incorporated into therapeutic substances.

Recombinant soluble receptors: Synthetic versions of cellular receptors manufactured with recombinant DNA technology, used as decoys to attract pathogens that otherwise would bind to cellular receptors and cause disease.

Ribonucleic Acid (RNA): A molecule similar to DNA that is used to help decode the genetic information in DNA.

Single nucleotide polymorphism (SNP): A variation in the sequence of a gene due to a change in a single nucleotide.

Technology transfer: The process of transferring discoveries made by basic research scientists in universities and government laboratories to the commercial sector for development into products and services.

Therapeutics: Drugs that are used to treat specific medical conditions or diseases.

Tissue plasminogen activator (TPA): A substance produced in small amounts by the inner lining of blood vessels, TPA prevents abnormal blood clotting by converting plasminogen, a chemical in the blood, to the enzyme plasmin.

Trademarks: An insignia or logo that distinguishes one maker's products from those of all others. Trademarks are used to protect company names, mottos, tag lines, and product names.

Transcription: The process by which information in a DNA sequence is used to construct an mRNA molecule.

Translation: The process by which information in mRNA is used to construct proteins.

Treatment IND: An FDA program that allows experimental drugs treating life-threatening illnesses to be made commercially available to very sick patients before the drugs obtain formal FDA approval.

Visit Vault at **www.vault.com** for insider company profiles, expert advice, career message boards, expert resume reviews, the Vault Job Board and more.

VAULT CAREER LIBRARY   **163**

Tumor necrosis factors (TNF): Rare proteins of the immune system that appear to destroy some types of tumor cells without affecting healthy cells.

Vector: Self-replicating DNA molecule (e.g., a plasmid or virus) that transfers a DNA segment between host cells.

Venture capital (VC): Source of financing for start-up companies or others embarking on new businesses that entail some investment risk but promise above-average future profits.

White blood cells: Cells that help the body fight infection and disease.

Wild type: The form of an organism that occurs most frequently in nature.

Yeast: A general term for single-cell fungi that reproduce by budding.

Sources:
- *Standard & Poor Industry Surveys*
- *The American Medical Association Home Medical Encyclopedia (American Medical Association)*
- *Biotechnology Medicines in Development (Pharmaceutical Research and Manufacturers of America)*
- *Guide to Biotechnology (Biotechnology Industry Organization)*
- *Massachusetts Biotechnology Council*
- *Dictionary of Business Terms*
- *The Entrepreneur's Guide to a Biotech Start-up*
- *Understanding Biotechnology*
- *Bioinformatics*

Recruiters

Biotechnology information directory

The Web Virtual Library, Employment, Recruitment, and Contract Staffing Link

Links to dozens of biotech and pharmaceutical recruiters and employers

http://www.cato.com/biotech/bio-employ.html

Clinical research, data management, and regulatory affairs recruiters

Advanced Clinical Services: Full-service, national staffing firm specializing in clinical research and data management for Phase I-IV trials, including contract, contract-to-hire, and direct hire options. www.advancedclinical.com

ASG: Consulting, outsourcing, and contract technical assistance in clinical trials. www.asg-inc.com

Biotech Resources: Clinical and manufacturing recruiting. www.biotechresources.net

ClinicalTrialJobs.com: Clinical research employment opportunities. www.clinicaltrialjobs.com

DrugDev123.com: Open positions in clinical research around the world. www.drugdev123.com

JAS Associates: Recruitment and placement of personnel working in clinical trials for pharmaceutical and biotech companies and contract research organizations. www.jasrecruiters.com

MedExec Intl.: Pharmaceutical, medical device, biotechnology, diagnostic, and biologicals industry clients through placement in clinical research, medical affairs, regulatory affairs, quality, and engineering departments. www.medexecintl.com

MonitorForHire.com: Contract monitors (CRAs). www.monitorforhire.com

Pharmaceutical Careers Inc.: Career opportunities in clinical research. www.pharmaceuticalcareers.com

Regsource: Jobs particularly in regulatory affairs but also in many other areas of pharmaceutical and device development. www.regsourcejobs.com

Target Consulting Services: Clinical research staffing. www.targetconsultingservices.com

The Woolf Group: Clinical research staffing organization offering contract and direct staffing solutions nationwide. www.thewoolfgroup.com

Life sciences disciplines and bioinformatics recruiters

BiologyJobs.com: Targeted resource for job seekers and employers interested in the life sciences. www.biologyjobs.com

http://www.biotech-recruiters.com: Contingency and retained recruitment in drug discovery and biotechnology

CastleRock Technology: Focus on biotech, R&D and pharmaceutical companies. www.crti.com

Evolution Recruitment Consultants: Specialists in biotechnology; areas of expertise include genomics, proteomics, bioinformatics, and business development. www.evolutionconsultants.com

futurebiojobs: Jobs in genomics, bioinformatics, proteomics, BioMEMs and microfluidics. www.futurebiojobs.com

GenomeJobs: Genomics, bioinformatics, biotechnology and biocomputing. www.genomejobs.com

Harcourt and Associates. Professional search firm specializing in biotech and technical placements. www.harcourt.ca

Northstar Agents. Executive search for bioinformatics and cheminformatics. www.northstaragents.com

http://www.rlassociatesinc.net: Scientific staffing for the biotechnology industry.

ResearchCareers.com: Focus on pharmaceutical and biotech research industry employment. www.researchcareers.com

ScienceJobs: Free science career site for job seekers listing industry, academic, and government bioscience employment opportunities from the scientific publishers, Cell, BioMedNet, and New Scientist. www.sciencejobs.com

Twin-Image Recruiting: Recruitment and placement of pharmaceutical research personnel for pharmaceutical, CRO, and biotech companies. www.twin-images.com

Biotech sales and marketing recruiters

Global Edge Recruiting Associates: Pharmaceutical, biotech, medical device, and medical sales industries. www.globaledgerecruiting.com

Innovative Medical Recruiting: Specializes in biotech, medical, and pharmaceutical sales and marketing professionals. www.innomedical.com

K.L. Williams: Recruiter focusing on senior sales, sales management, marketing, applications, business development, and marketing communications in biotech and biopharmaceuticals. www.isearchbio.com

Medical Sales Associates: National recruiters for sales professionals in the pharmaceutical and medical sectors. www.msajobs.com

Seltek Consultants: Technical sales positions in the life sciences, biotechnology, molecular biology, chemistry, diagnostics, immunology, and instrumentation industries. www.seltekconsultants.co.uk

Advertising and communications recruiters

Careers Front Page: Opportunities in biotechnology, pharmaceutical advertising, and medical communications. www.shsinc.com

Full-service recruiters

Albrecht Associates: Executive search in biotechnology and pharmaceuticals. www.albrecht-assoc.com

Aerotek Scientific: Full service staffing firm; contains job search site at http://www.thingamajob.com

BioCareer Center: Career opportunities courtesy of Biotechnology Industry Organization (BIO) and SciWeb ("The Life Science Home Page"). www.biocareer.com

BioExchange: Bio-pharmaceutical network integrating community, a career board, e-commerce, and industry-specific tools and resources. www.bioexchange.com

Visit Vault at **www.vault.com** for insider company profiles, expert advice, career message boards, expert resume reviews, the Vault Job Board and more.

VAULT CAREER LIBRARY   **167**

BioJobNet: Network for biotechnology, pharmaceutical and life sciences industries. www.biojobnet.com

Bio Online Career Center: Comprehensive web resource site for the biological sciences. www.bio.com

Biotech Career Center: Employment opportunities, news, and links. http://biotech.deep13.com

BioView: An easy-to-use link to today's life sciences employment resources for employees and employers alike. www.bioview.com

BioWorks: Biotechnology, biomedicine, and bioengineering recruiting. www.bioworksinc.com

Bob Gammon Associates. Careers in healthcare and pharmaceutical development. www.bobgammon.com

The Bowdoin Group: Recruitment in pharmaceuticals, biotechnology, and medical industries. www.bowdoingroup.com

job-hunt.org: Medical, biotechnology, and pharmaceutical job listings. www.job-hunt.org

Jobscience: Jobs in biotech, medical device, diagnostics, and pharmaceuticals. www.jobscience.net

MedZilla: Jobs in biotechnology, pharmaceuticals, science, medicine, and healthcare. www.medzilla.com

National Search Associates (NSA): Executive search and recruitment in biotechnology/pharmaceuticals, software development, and medical devices. www.nsasearch.com

SP Associates: Pharmaceuticals, medical devices and biotechnology. www.spassociates.com

Groups and Organizations

The Biotechnology Industry Organization (BIO): A leading industry group.

1225 Eye St., NW, Suite 1100
Washington, D.C. 20005 USA
Phone: (202) 962-9200
Fax: (202) 962-9201
Web site: http://www.bio.org

National Biotech Register: An online guide to biopharmaceutical companies indexed by keyword to provide real-time information to academics, business people in the industry

PO Box 551
Wilmington, MA 01887-0551
Phone: (978) 658-0442
Fax: (978) 657-869
Web site: http://biotech-register.com/

Online Resources

Biotechnology Information Directory of the Web Virtual Library: A directory of over 1,500 links to companies, research institutes, universities, sources of information, and other directories specific to biopharmaceutical product development and delivery of products and services. www.vlib.org

BioMedNet: Provides useful links to thousands of biological Web sites. http://www.links.bmn.com

Bio.com: Resource for biotechnology news, analysis and Webcasts. http://www.bio.com

Biospace.com: Hub site for bioscience-specific news, information, and links on biotechnology and pharmaceutical developments. http://www.biospace.com

Signals: The online magazine of Biotechnology Industry Analysis Recombinant Capital: Database on strategic alliances, product development, and company-specific information. http://www.recap.com

FierceBiotech: The Biotech Industry's Daily Monitor: Daily bulletin on biotech industry news http://www.FierceBiotech

BioWorld Online: Worldwide biotechnology news and information resource
3525 Piedmont Road
Building 6, Suite 400
Atlanta, GA 30305
Web site: http://www.bioworld.com
In the U.S. and Canada: 1 (800) 688-2421
Outside the U.S.: 1 (404) 262-5476

Evelexa BioResources: Business and career-related information for those interested in biotech venture creation. Also the home of The Entrepreneur's Guide to a Biotech Startup.

Peter Kolchinsky, Ph.D.
Director
Phone: (617) 320-8789
Fax: (617) 444-8505
245 First St., 18th Floor
Cambridge, MA 02142

E-mail: info2@evelexa.com
Web site: http://www.evelexa.com

BiotechFind: Directory of international links covering biotechnologies and biofinances; includes a biotechnology career center.
http://www.BiotechFind.com

Bioinformatics sites: Organization for bioinformatics professionals.
http://www.bioinformatics.org

National Center for Biotechnology Information: The National Center for Biotechnology Information is a resource for public databases and bioinformatics tools and applications.
http://www.ncbi.nlm.nih.gov

Government Agencies

Centers for Disease Control and Prevention: Federal agency mandated to prevent and contain diseases through partnerships, monitoring, and information access.

U.S. Dept. of Health and Human Services
1600 Clifton Rd.
Atlanta, GA 30333
Phone: (404) 639-3311
Web site: http://www.cdc.gov

Food and Drug Administration (FDA): Federal agency mandated to supervise the food, pharmaceutical, and biotechnology industries.

5600 Fishers Lane
Rockville, MD 20857
Phone: (301) 827-5006
Web site: http://www.fda.gov

National Center for Health Statistics (NCHS): Principal vital and health statistics agency for the U.S. government.

U.S. Dept. of Health and Human Services
6525 Belcrest Rd.
Hyattsville, MD 20782
Phone: (301) 458-4636
Web site: http://www.cdc.gov/nchs

National Institutes of Health (NIH): Leading medical research center, the NIH conducts research in its own laboratories and supports research by scientists in universities, medical schools, hospitals, and research institutions in the U.S. and abroad.

U.S. Dept. of Health and Human Services
9000 Rockville Pike
Bethesda, MD 20892
Web site: http://www.nih.gov

Visit Vault at **www.vault.com** for insider company profiles, expert advice, career message boards, expert resume reviews, the Vault Job Board and more.

VAULT CAREER LIBRARY 173

State Biotechnology Councils

Biotechnology Association of Alabama
Mr. Michael Alder
Executive Director
500 Beacon Parkway West
Birmingham, AL 35209
Phone: (205) 943-5124
Fax: (205) 943-4748
Web site: www.bioalabama.com
E-mail: malder@redmontvp.com

Arizona Bioindustry Cluster
Ms. Eileen Walker
Associate Director
ASU Research Park, 8750 S. Science Dr.
Tempe, AZ 85284-2603
Phone: (480) 752-2016
Fax: (480) 491-2273
Web site: www.azbiocluster.org
E-mail: eileen.walker@asu.edu

**Arkansas Biotechnology Association
c/o UAMS College of Medicine**
Ms. Alice Rumph Smith
Executive Director
4301 W Markham St.
Little Rock, AR 72205-7101
Phone: (501) 686-5393
Fax: (501) 686-5873
Web site:
www.biotech.uams.edu/aba/aba.html
E-mail: smithalicer@uams.edu

BayBio
Ms. Caitlyn Waller
President
651 Gateway Boulevard, Suite 1145
South San Francisco, CA 94080
Phone: (650) 871-7101
Fax: (650) 871-7555
Web site: www.baybio.org
E-mail: cwaller@baybio.org

BIOCOM/San Diego
Mr. Joseph D. Panetta
President & CEO
4510 Executive Drive, Plaza One
San Diego, CA 92121
Phone: (858) 455-0300
Fax: (858) 455-0022
Web site: www.biocom.org
E-mail: jpanetta@biocom.org

California Healthcare Institute
Ms. Cristin Lis
VP, Public Policy
1020 Prospect Street, Suite 310
La Jolla, CA 92037
Phone: (858) 551-6677
Fax: (858) 551-6688
Web site: www.chi.org
E-mail: lis@chi.org

Visit Vault at **www.vault.com** for insider company profiles, expert advice,
career message boards, expert resume reviews, the Vault Job Board and more.

VAULT CAREER LIBRARY   175

Southern California Biomedical Council
Mr. Ahmed A. Enany
Executive Director
515 South Flower Street, 32nd Floor
Los Angeles, CA 90071
Phone: (213) 236-4890
Fax: (213) 622-7100
Web site: www.socalbio.org
E-mail: enany@socalbio.org

Colorado Biotechnology Association
Ms. Denise Brown
Executive Director
12635 East Montview Boulevard, Suite 127
Aurora, CO 80010
Phone: (720) 859-4153
Fax: (720) 859-4110
Web site: www.cobiotech.com
E-mail: dbrown@colobio.com

Connecticut United for Research Excellence, Inc. (CURE)
Mr. Paul Pescatello
President
300 George Street, Suite 541
New Haven, CT 06511
Phone: (203) 777-8747
Fax: (203) 777-8754
Web site: www.curenet.org
E-mail: ppescatello@curenet.org

Delaware BioScience Association
Mr. Michael Strine
Executive Director
1201 N Orange St., Suite 200
Wilmington, DE 19801-1155
Phone: (302) 576-6590
Fax: (302) 654-0691
E-mail: mstrine@dscc.com

BioFlorida
Mr. Paul Hassie
President
5547 SW 37th Drive
Gainseville, FL 32608
Phone: (352) 371-1728
Fax: (352) 371-6387
Web site: www.bioflorida.com
E-mail: phassie@bioflorida.com

Georgia Biomedical Partnership, Inc.
Mr. John Spencer, Jr.
President
1199 Euclid Avenue, NE
Atlanta, GA 30307
Phone: (404) 221-0617
Fax: (404) 522-0132
Web site: www.gabio.org
E-mail: jack.spencer@gabio.org

Hawaii Biotechnology Council
Mr. David Watumull
Chairman
3661-A Woodlawn Dr.
Honolulu, HI 96822
Phone: (808) 988-6580
Fax: (808) 988-5816
E-mail: watumull@lava.net

Illinois Biotechnology Industry Organization
Mr. David Miller
President
177 N State St., Suite 500
Chicago, IL 60601-3623
Phone: (312) 201-4519
Fax: (312) 553-4355
Web site: www.ibio.org
E-mail: info@ibio.org

Indiana Health Industry Forum

Mr. Wade A. Lange
President & CEO
351 W 10th St., Suite 216
Indianapolis, IN 46202-4118
Phone: (317) 278-9970
Fax: (317) 278-9971
Web site: www.ihif.org
E-mail: ihif@ihif.org

Iowa Biotechnology Association

Mr. Doug Getter
Executive Director
4536 NW 114th Street, Suite A
Urbandale, IA 50322
Phone: (515) 327-9156
Fax: (515) 327-1407
Web site: www.iowabiotech.org
E-mail: dgetter@netins.net

KansasBIO c/o Kansas Technology Enterprise Corporation

214 SW 6th Ave., First Floor
Topeka, KS 66603-3719
Phone: (785) 296-3363
Fax: (785) 296-1160
Web site: www.kansasbio.org

Kentucky Life Sciences Organization

Mr. Will Montague
Secretary
300 W Vine St., Suite 2100
Lexington, KY 40507-1621
Phone: (859) 231-3946
Fax: (859) 253-1093
Web site: www.klso.com
E-mail: wlm2@skp.com

Biotechnology Association of Maine

Ms. Cheryl Timberlake
Executive Director
P.O. Box 615, 150 Capitol Street
August, ME 04332-0615
Phone: (207) 623-3790
Fax: (207) 621-0175
Web site: www.mainebiotech.org
E-mail:
ctimberlake@capitolinsights.com

Maryland Bioscience Alliance Technology Council of Maryland

Mr. Matt Gardner
Director
9700 Great Seneca Highway
Rockville, MD 20850
Phone: (240) 453-6221
Fax: (240) 453-6201
Web site:
www.mdhitech.org/networks/bioalliance
.html
E-mail: mgardner@mdhitech.org

Massachusetts Biotechnology Council (MBC)

Ms. Janice Bourque
President & CEO
One Cambridge Center, 9th Floor
Cambridge, MA 02142
Phone: (617) 577-8198
Fax: (617) 577-7860
Web site: www.massbio.org
E-mail: janice_bourque@massbio.org

Visit Vault at www.vault.com for insider company profiles, expert advice,
career message boards, expert resume reviews, the Vault Job Board and more.

VAULT CAREER LIBRARY   177

MichBio
Mr. Michael Witt
Executive Director
2232 South Main Street, Suite 452
Ann Arbor, MI 48103
Phone: (734) 944-6241
Fax: (734) 944-1065
Web site: www.michbio.org
E-mail: michael@michbio.org

Minnesota Biotechnology Association (MNBIO)
Mr. Ray Frost
Executive Director
26 Exchange St. E., Suite 500
Saint Paul, MN 55101-1671
Phone: (651) 290-6286
Fax: (651) 290-2266
Web site: www.minnesotabiotech.org
E-mail: rayf@ewald.com

Missouri Biotechnology Association
Mr. Bill Romjue
Executive Director
102 E High St, Suite 200
Jefferson City, MO 65101-5406
Phone: (573) 636-5252
Fax: (573) 636-5363
Web site: www.mobio.org

New Hampshire Biotechnology Center
Lulu Pickering Ph.D.
President
PO Box 279
Greenland, NH 03840-0279
Phone: (603) 436-2552
Fax: (603) 427-1327
Web site: www.nhbiotech.com
E-mail: pickering@nhbiotech.com

Biotechnology Council of New Jersey
Ms. Debbie Hart
President
1 AAA Drive, Suite 102
Trenton, NJ 08691
Phone: (609) 890-3185
Fax: (609) 581-8244
Web site: www.newjerseybiotech.org
E-mail: dhart@hq4u.com

New Mexico Biotechnology and Biomedical Assoc. c/o Peacock, Myers & Adams, P.C.
Ms. Marcia Nass
Board Member
201 3rd St. NW, Ste. 1340
Albuquerque, NM 87102-3370
Phone: (505) 998-6124
Fax: (505) 243-2542
Web site: www.nmbio.org
E-mail: mnass@peacocklaw.com

New York Biotechnology Association
Ms. Karin Duncker
Executive Director
666 Third Avenue, 24th Floor
New York, NY 10017
Phone: (212) 661-1780
Fax: (631) 444-8895
Web site: www.nyba.org
E-mail: kduncker@mindspring.com

North Carolina Biosciences Organization
Mr. Sam Taylor
Executive Director
4220 Knightsbridge Way
Raleigh, NC 27604-8440
Phone: (919) 212-1833
Fax: (919) 212-1885
E-mail: samuelmtaylor@earthlink.net

Omeris Inc.
Mr. Tony Dennis
President
1275 Kinnear Rd
Columbus, OH 43212-1155
Phone: (614) 675-3686
Fax: (614) 615-3687
Web site: www.omeris.org
E-mail: tony_dennis@ebtc.org

Oregon Biosciences Association
Ms. Barbara Anderman
Director, Operations
222 NW 5th Avenue, Suite 304
Portland, OR 97209
Phone: (503) 228-5401
Fax: (503) 228-5411
Web site: www.oregon-bioscience.com
E-mail: barbara@sao.org

Pennsylvania Biotechnology Association
Mr. Fritz Bittenbender
President
20 Valley Stream Parkway, Suite 265
Malvern, PA 19355-1457
Phone: (610) 578-9220
Fax: (610) 578-9219
Web site: www.pabiotech.org
E-mail: fbittenbender@pabiotech.org

Palmetto Biotechnology Alliance
Mr. Karl Kelly
Interim Executive Director
1 Gregor Mendel Circle, Building D
Greenwood, SC 29646-2307
Phone: (864) 953-3980
Fax: (864) 953-3984
E-mail: kkelly@ggc.org

Tennessee Biotechnology Association
Ms. Caroline Young
Executive Director
312 8th Avenue North, 9th floor
Nashville, TN 37243
Phone: (615) 253-1760
Fax: (615) 253-6443
Web site: www.tnbio.org
E-mail: cyoung@tnbio.org

Texas Healthcare & Bioscience Institute
Mr. Thomas Kowalski
President
815 Brazos, Suite 310
Austin, TX 78701
Phone: (512) 708-8424
Fax: (512) 708-1607
Web site: www.thbi.com
E-mail: tk@thbi.com

Utah Life Science Association
Mr. Brian H. Moss
President
P.O. Box 58073
Salt Lake City, UT 84158-0073
Phone: (801) 584-1111
Fax: (801) 584-1119
Web site: www.utahlifescience.com
E-mail: ulsa@xmission.com

Virginia Biotechnology Association
Mr. Mark A. Herzog
Executive Director
800 East Leigh Street, Suite 14
Richmond, VA 23219
Phone: (804) 643-6360
Fax: (804) 643-6361
Web site: www.vabio.org
E-mail: mherzog@vabio.org

Visit Vault at **www.vault.com** for insider company profiles, expert advice,
career message boards, expert resume reviews, the Vault Job Board and more.

VAULT CAREER LIBRARY   179

**Washington Biotechnology &
Biomedical Association**
Ms. Ruth Scott
President
200 First Avenue West, Suite 200
Seattle, WA 98101
Phone: (206) 624-1967
Fax: (206) 628-0899
Web site: www.wabio.com
E-mail: ruths@washbio.org

**Wisconsin Biotechnology Association
c/o DeWitt Ross & Stevens S.C.**
Mr. James Leonhardt
Executive VP
2 East Mifflin Street, Suite 600
Madison, WI 53703
Phone: (608) 252-9393
Fax: (608) 283-5508
Web site: www.wisconsinbiotech.org
E-mail: info@wisconsinbiotech.org

International Biotech
Organizations

Australia

AusBiotech, formerly the Australian Biotechnology Association, is the national body of companies and individuals dedicated to the development and prosperity of the Australian biotechnology industry.

AusBiotech Ltd.
576 Swan Street.
Richmond, Vic 3121 Australia
Phone: 01-16-1392084204
Fax: 01-16-1392084201
Web site: www.ausbiotech.org
Contact: Anthony Coulepis, Executive Director
E-mail: agcoulepis@ausbiotech.org

Brazil

ABRABI – Associacao Brasileira de Empresas de Biotechnologia
Av. 13 de Maio sl 1301
Rio de Janeiro, RJ CEP20031-910 Brazil
Phone: 01-15-52122201109
Fax: 01-15-52122201109
Contact: Joao de S.B. Paes de Carvalho, Executive Director
E-mail: jsbpc@abrabi.org.br

Canada

BIOTECanada is the national organization dedicated to promoting a better understanding of biotechnology and the many ways it contributes to improving the quality of life of all Canadians.

Visit Vault at **www.vault.com** for insider company profiles, expert advice, career message boards, expert resume reviews, the Vault Job Board and more.

VAULT CAREER LIBRARY 181

BIOTECanada
420 – 130 Albert Street
Ottawa, ON K1P 5G4 Canada
Phone: (613) 230-5585
Fax: (613) 563-8850
Web site: www.biotech.ca
Contact: Charlene Winchester,
Executive Assistant
E-mail: charlene@biotech.ca

India

All India Biotech Association
Vipps Centre 2 , Local Shopping Centre Block-EFGH, Masjid Moth, G.K-II
New Delhi 110048 India
Phone: 01-10-916430546
Fax: 01-10-916469166
Web site: www.aibaonline.com

Ireland

The Irish BioIndustry Association (IBIA) is the leading representative body for the
Biotech Industry in Ireland. The association has 40 member companies and is
affiliated with the Irish Business and Employers Association.

Irish Bioindustry Association
84/86 Lower Baggot Street .
Dublin 2 Ireland
Phone: 01-13-5316051567
Fax: 01-13-5316381567
Web site: www.ibec.ie
Contact: Matt Moran, Director
E-mail: matt.moran@ibec.ie

Japan

JBA is a non-profit organization dedicated to the promotion of bioscience, biotechnology, and bioindustry in both Japan and the rest of the world.

Japan Bioindustry Association
Grande Building 8F 26-9, Hatchobori 2-chome
Chuo-ku, Tokyo 104 Japan
Phone: 01-18-1355412731
Fax: 01-18-1355412737
Contact: Tadashi Hirakawa
E-mail: hirakawa@jba.or.jp

South Africa

AfricaBio is an independent, non-political, non-profit biotechnology stakeholders association serving as a factual reference point and forum for informed dialogue on biotechnological issues.

AFRICABIO Biotechnology Stakeholders Association
P.O. Box 873, Irene Centurion
Guateng 0062 South Africa
Phone: 01-12-7126672689
Fax: 01-12-7126671920
Web site: www.africabio.com
Contact: Jocelyn Webster, Executive Director
E-mail: africabio@mweb.co.za

South Korea

Bioindustry Association of Korea
16th Floor, F.K.I. Building 28-1 Yoido-Dong Yongdungpo-Ku
Seoul 150-756 Republic of Korea
Phone: 011-82-2-761-3176
Fax: 011-82-2-780-3524
Web site: www.bak.or.kr

United Kingdom

The BioIndustry Association (BIA) is the trade association for over 450 innovative enterprises in the U.K.'s bioscience sector.

BIA – BioIndustry Association
14-15 Belgrave Square
London SW1X 8PS United Kingdom
Phone: 01-14-42075657190
Fax: 01-14-42075657191
Web site: www.bioindustry.org
Contact: Dr. Samia Saad, Business Development Manager
E-mail: ssaad@bioindustry.org

Source: The Bio Organization

Recommended Reading

Periodicals

The Biotechnology Industry Annual Report
http://www.burrillandco.com

BioCentury: The Bernstein Report on BioBusiness
http://www.biocentury.com

BioWorld Today

BioWorld Week

BioWorld Biotechnology State of the Industry Report
http://www.bioworld.com

F-D-C Reports: The Pink Sheet
http://www.fdcreports.com

Genetic Engineering News
http://www.genengnews.com

MedAdNews
http://www.pharmalive.com

Modern Drug Discovery
http://pubs.acs.org/journals/mdd/index.html

Nature Biotechnology
http://www.nature.com/nbt

New England Journal of Medicine
http://www.nejm.org

PARAXEL's Pharmaceutical R&D Statistical Sourcebook
http://www.paraxel.com

PharmaBusiness
http://www.pharmalive.com

Books

Borem, Aluzio; Santos, Fabricio R.; and Bowen, David E. *Understanding Biotechnology*. Prentice Hall/PTR, 2003; 216 pages; ISBN: 0131010115

Brown, Sheldon S. and Rowh, Mark. *Opportunities in Biotechnology Careers.* McGraw-Hill/Contemporary Books, 2000; 160 pages; ISBN: 0658004808.

Camenson, Blythe; Lambert, Stephen E; and Degalan, Julie Ann. Great Jobs for Biology Majors. McGraw-Hill/Contemporary Books, 1999; 272 pages; ISBN: 0844219177.

Simon, F.; Kotler, P.; and Sharer, K. *Building Global Biobrands: Taking Biotechnology to Market*, The Free Press, 2003; 336 pages; ISBN: 074322244X.

Westhead, D.R.; Parish, J.H.; and Twyman, R.M. *Bioinformatics*. BIOS Scientific Publishers, Ltd., 2002; 257 pages; ISBN: 1859962726.

About the Author

Carole Moussalli

Carole Moussalli has been a consultant in information design/delivery and professional development for Fortune 1000 clients in several industries, including pharmaceuticals and biotech. She earned an MS in Organic Chemistry from the University of North Carolina.

Visit Vault at **www.vault.com** for insider company profiles, expert advice, career message boards, expert resume reviews, the Vault Job Board and more.

VAULT CAREER LIBRARY   **187**